UNFORGETTABLE *Gifts*

Book 9 Reflections of God Moments

Dedication

Gifts come in all shapes and sizes. Some are tangible and others intangible. I am blessed to have gotten to have siblings in my life who have blessed me with nieces and nephews that I get to watch grow and become as I watch my own children. I dedicate this book to legacy: the unforgettable gift of life given by God; my parent's gift of life to me and my siblings; and the gift of love that continues to grow through choosing life.

Unforgettable Gifts
Book 9 Reflections of God Moments
copyright © 2024

Written by: Donesa Walker
Design by: Will Baten
Edited by: Kelley Inderman

He who pampers his servant from childhood Will have him as a son in the end. An angry man stirs up strife, And a furious man abounds in transgression. A man's pride will bring him low, But the humble in spirit will retain honor. The fear of man brings a snare, But whoever trusts in the Lord shall be safe.
Proverbs 29:21-23, 25

If you let people treat you like a doormat, you'll be quite forgotten in the end. Angry people stir up a lot of discord; the intemperate stir up trouble. Pride lands you flat on your face; humility prepares you for honors. The fear of human opinion disables; trusting in God protects you from that.
Proverbs 29:21-23, 25

DOORMATS OF PRIDE!

Interpretations of scripture can vary and it is important to look at various versions because the outcome or takeaway can be vastly different. Opinions matter, interpretations matter but what matters more is God's viewpoint. Man wrote scripture that was God inspired and recorded it. Other men decided what should/shouldn't be included in various versions and translations but when reading any scripture, only God can open our eyes. Here are two interpretations of the exact same scriptures, both translated from the original language but quite different in their outcome especially in the first verse. One says that a man who treats his servant well ends up with him as a son and another interprets the scripture negatively to say if people treat you as a doormat, you will be forgotten. This is exactly how interpreting can cause miscommunication, confusion/conflict in our lives. Anger, pride and fear cause us to forget our place on the wall with God. It was pride that caused the sin to enter the world then fear from the fall caused by that pride led to hiding from God which ultimately allowed anger to create a chasm between God/man. Jesus bridged this divide. God pampered us as His servants and we began to be ungrateful for His largesse as we saw our role as His child and forgot the role of His servant. Yes, God has raised us up through His goodness but we forget our place when we begin to think we outsmart the Creator himself. When we take on the role of sons/daughters, it does not preempt the role of servant. Anger, pride, and fear of the opinions of men have driven us away from realizing that our role as children of God is through the role of servant-hood. Jesus took on the role of man to become a servant of all so that we could know and understand the wisdom of the ages. We are not doormats who have to worry about whether we will be forgotten when we remember who we are in the eyes of a king who was willing to lay down His own life for us. We are children of the king willing to serve Him. Anger and strife only stir up trouble and pride, which, when we feel we've been offended, brings us low. Take a step back. Both of these pictures are the same, just taken at a different step or focus. When you feel you are wronged or your pride has been injured, take a step back. Don't let the fear of being rejected or wronged tear you down. Don't let pride bring you to your knees. Instead, call upon the Lord and trust that He will make things right. Take a step back and refocus your energies and thoughts on Him. Then you can see the true beauty of the rose held up by the living water, Supported by the unseen hand and glorious in its appearance because of the spirit of life that surrounds it. Fear brings a trap, pride brings a fall and anger brings strife. Isn't it time to let these go in servanthood and allow the King of Glory to pamper you into the role of His son instead of you feeling like you are a doormat? It's all about trusting who He is and getting away from human opinion into the only perspective that matters-His. I trust Him to lead me each day as I walk just as He in His wisdom is able to open the rose.

Therefore I remind you to stir up the gift of God which is in you through the laying on of my hands. For God has not given us a spirit of fear, but of power and of love and of a sound mind.

Hold fast the pattern of sound words which you have heard from me, in faith and love which are in Christ Jesus. That good thing which was committed to you, keep by the Holy Spirit who dwells in us.

2 Timothy 1: 6-7, 13-14

STIR UP THE GIFT!

I was thirsty and excitedly poured myself a glass of freshly made tea only to notice the flavor was off. I realized quickly that the tea had not been stirred. The ingredients were all there, sitting in the same container but not mixed so their flavors would compliment one another. The sugar/Sucralose rested on the bottom with the water in the middle and the strong tea straight from the coffee pot on top so I got only the strong tea flavor without the things that make it palatable. Paul instructed Timothy in this passage to stir up the gift of God in himself like a fire. A fire burns hot then as the wood burns down, the heat goes into the coals or the remaining portion of wood to hold. When you add more fuel, no fire grabs onto it unless you stir the fire up so the heat can reach the fuel. Much like my tea, the sweetness of the gospel and the living water must be stirred up with the good solid truths so that it can be fully absorbed. God didn't give us a spirit of fear of our future but hope which is in His power, His love and His strength so that we can combat the evil that is sent to cloud our thinking. It is easy for fear to grab hold of us when we listen to the constant barrage of negativity that flows through society in televised ways to streaming data on social media. Timothy was experiencing this too as he received news of his brother preachers being jailed for sharing the gospel. Paul reminded him not to be diluted by the things around him but to hold to the pattern of soundness. Today, we experience a constant barrage of lies about who God is through various sources that have diluted the gospel into their own religion so they can flavor their experiences to their own making. The reality is that diluting the gospel undermines the good flavor and changes it until it is unrecognizable. I like flavors in my tea. I especially love mint tea with a little blackberry flavor or peach tea with a little mango but if you put too much, the original flavor is lost and hidden. God's truth is recorded in His word and although there are various translations and changes over the centuries, the power of the truth is in the pattern of soundness. When the pattern is lost, the replica is not true. The good thing, the pattern is kept true in us through the Holy Spirit who dwells in us. The faith and love of Christ stirred up in us becomes the wonderful answer to those around us who need to see God's power and truth in the confusion of today. Stir it up in us so that the sweetness and the flavor of His truth mix together in a thirst quench. Then the pattern of His truth guides us into His power and might so we can stand against all that is thrown against us.

Jesus told this simple story, but they had no idea what he was talking about. So he tried again. "I'll be explicit, then. I am the Gate for the sheep. All those others are up to no good—sheep rustlers, every one of them. But the sheep didn't listen to them. I am the Gate. Anyone who goes through me will be cared for—will freely go in and out, and find pasture. A thief is only there to steal and kill and destroy. I came so they can have real and eternal life, more and better life than they ever dreamed of.
John 10:6-10

THE GATE!

Yesterday I watched a little boy try to get himself through a closed gate when he had no idea how to open it but wanted on the other side badly. He stuck his hand through, his foot and leg. He fussed and squalled but his family was not about to open the gate because they knew the danger on the other side. Then a few hours later, I watched another young boy attempt to open a gate when his hands were full managing a 4 wheeler. If he got off the machine to open the gate, the machine shut off for safety. He got the gate open but had to hold it open with his body and couldn't get the machine through. Both of these boys felt a little like I did in the pouring rain last week as I tried to no avail to get my gate opener to work. I had to get out in the cold pouring rain to reset the gate so I could use the code I knew worked. Jesus is our gate of safety and direction. He knows, even though we think we want something, what is or isn't good for us, for He can see the dangers. Jesus is our gate of direction and He knows that we shouldn't bring into our lives the things that will distract from Him so He makes us choose by not allowing the gate to remain open to permit all. He has a set of standards that must be met. Jesus is our gate and sometimes we need to reset our lives in the focus on Him so that the gate opener of prayer is heard and acknowledged. In John, Jesus told a simple story of the Gate (Jesus) and the sheep (people). He explained that He is the Gate that protects and provides pasture. He gives freedom to the people/sheep but protects them from the thief that would steal, kill and destroy. I chose this picture because this past week, Satan came to steal, kill and destroy marriages and families. He knows his time is limited and he is rampaging around like a roaring lion seeking whom he may devour. Those of us who were safely inside the Gate but sticking our hands and feet through got some scrapes and bruises while others who tried to hold the gate open to things not of God were disappointed that they cannot have it both ways and were forced to make a decision. Others of us had to get a hard reset in the midst of a storm because we hadn't paid attention that the battery of our love life was running low. Jesus is the Gate to a better life than we have ever dreamed of, a more life, a rich life and a full of love life. Jesus is the Gate and we His people need to ignore the rustlers and stay in the fence of His love. We should reach out through the gate to those hurting to draw them in but we cannot have it both ways. Jesus is the Gate and we are either in or out. We have freedom to choose, but choose, we must. He directs us like a caring parent away from danger by blocking things that would lead to our destruction. He cares for us. Jesus is the Gate to eternal life. Just as the trees in this photo twine together to form a heart, so should we be entwined with Jesus.

Now that we are set right with God by means of this sacrificial death, the consummate blood sacrifice, there is no longer a question of being at odds with God in any way. If, when we were at our worst, we were put on friendly terms with God by the sacrificial death of his Son, now that we're at our best, just think of how our lives will expand and deepen by means of his resurrection life! Now that we have actually received this amazing friendship with God, we are no longer content to simply say it in plodding prose. We sing and shout our praises to God through Jesus, the Messiah!

Romans 5: 9-11

FROM PLODDING TO PRAISING!

Set right. Two very powerful words that indicate someone did an amazing thing. The dishes were set right on the table, doesn't have near the same meaning as we are set right with God! Set right means that the bridge was firmed up across the abyss of sin. It was set right upon the cornerstone of God's love and Jesus' sacrificial death but the bridge itself came through the resurrection to life eternal. Most of us are born into this world screaming at the unjustness of being ejected from the womb. The moment we enter this world, our whole system feels the pressure of being at odds with God and born into a sin world. We are born with a demanding "all about me" spirit of sin from that first breath until we grasp the gift of servanthood through acceptance of the gift of life that Christ gave us. His sacrificial death takes our worst and converts it to God's best through His son. His blood of atonement covers the awkwardness of our sin and the horror of the judgment for that sin. God in us deepens and expands our lives into resurrection life. This is a life of joy, contentment and praise. Friendship with God is a certainty not a maybe. Oh that we really get this! We are no longer just plodding through our days, one moment to the next, trying to get through to the weekend, faking it until we make it...we are friends with God! I recently walked into a location I was invited to and felt a little awkward as I entered because it was a room full of strangers until the guest of honor saw me. At that moment, she beelined it to me, hugged me and suddenly I was the star of the moment wrapped in my friendship with the guest of honor. I was wrapped in her esteem and hugged by her presence which allowed me to shine in her glory for a moment. I was her honored friend held up by her in front of others. This is what Paul is expressing. We are no longer just going through the motions but now we have status and purpose. We are friends with the God of the Universe who speaks worlds into existence. Yea, you didn't get that because I didn't hear your excitement over here. When we truly grasp this, there is nothing to do except sing, dance, shout and praise. I have seen people win awards or special accolades with a plodding spirit and I have seen those who realize them in joy. We are friends of God Himself! When we grasp this fully, our lives will deepen like a hole in the ground accepting the vastness of a rain shower. The reign of God over lives is like a flooding rain over a grassy yard. At first, it changes the atmosphere then the ground is wet, then soggy then marshy then the water content of His love begins to overflow the capacity of the vessel to take it in so it forms a puddle then a pond then a lake then a deep well running like a river. From a plodding steady rain to a river teeming with life, this is our story. Set right! I am a friend of God! He calls me Friend!

I, John, am writing this to the seven churches in Asia province: All the best to you from The God Who Is, The God Who Was, and The God About to Arrive, and from the Seven Spirits assembled before his throne, and from Jesus Christ—Loyal Witness, Firstborn from the dead, Ruler of all earthly kings. Glory and strength to Christ, who loves us, who blood-washed our sins from our lives, Who made us a Kingdom, Priests for his Father, forever—and yes, he's on his way! Riding the clouds, he'll be seen by every eye, those who mocked and killed him will see him, People from all nations and all times will tear their clothes in lament. Oh, Yes. The Master declares, "I'm A to Z. I'm The God Who Is, The God Who Was, and The God About to Arrive. I'm the Sovereign-Strong."
Revelation 1:4-8

THE GOD WHO IS, WAS, COMING!

Anticipation! I love the Christmas season and all the anticipation as well as all the anticipation before a marriage or a birth. We have celebrations constantly as we await the day. Christ's return is foretold throughout scripture but made clear in full details in the book of Revelation. People get all bent out of shape because the exact day/time isn't foretold but the signs of the times are. Scripture compares His return as a thief coming in the night and the timing as an expected pregnancy. The earth is pregnant awaiting the birth/return of the Savior. First He came as an actual babe with an actual unexpected birth in a stable and now He will return as a conquering King at an unexpected time but in both cases the timing was foretold through signs that those paying attention could interpret. The God who was, we read about in scripture and the God who is, we can experience daily in all we do as we anticipate the God who is about to arrive. All three dimensions of Him are Him. The photo in this picture is an illustration of all of this. This photo may appear to be a cloud or a storm but it is really a babe in the womb on a sonogram photo. It is the photo of a child foretold through prophecy that happens in our world today. It is a photo of a long awaited birth. It is the photo of a cherished one who will change the lives of all those who surround the child and yet, the birth of this child will not save the lives of others. This birth is anticipated, longed for, prayed for, foretold and anxiously awaited and yet the parents nor others involved know the exact day/time. Celebrations have ensued as preparations are made ready. Announcements of gender and name and rooms made ready...all is being prepared. Why am I going on about this? Because this is the way we should be about Christ's return. We should be in breathless anticipation, celebrating, preparing, announcing and sharing with the world. We should be having all of those around us eager to herald His return for it is as certain as the birth of this baby. His return is as evident in the signs around us. His return is going to change the entire world and affect the lives of everyone we know. His return will be seen by all, known by all and declared by many. And yet, many lies will be told about His expected return. Many false news reports will be bandied about as this Loyal Witness and Ruler of all earthly kings who has made us a kingdom and washed our sins rides the glory clouds to bring us home. This Sovereign Strong God is coming and it is time for us to prepare. Who have you told? Who do you want to tell? Why haven't you told them? Why are you waiting? Jesus is coming soon. With a joyful heart, I await His returning.

And so I insist—and God backs me up on this—that there be no going along with the crowd, the empty-headed, mindless crowd. They've refused for so long to deal with God that they've lost touch not only with God but with reality itself. They can't think straight anymore. Feeling no pain, they let themselves go in sexual obsession, addicted to every sort of perversion. Watch the way you talk. Let nothing foul or dirty come out of your mouth. Say only what helps, each word a gift.

Ephesians 4: 17-19, 29

LOST TOUCH!

When I know you can, I trust you will. People everywhere are talking about things that happened recently that horrified their sensibilities from Super Bowl half-time shows to Grammy award shows to things posted in social media, but the truth is, there's nothing new under the sun. All of this has been going on for a very, very long time. Just look at this scripture in Ephesians as an example where Paul is writing a letter, telling the Ephesian people that God backs him up on the knowledge that going along with the crowd who are empty-headed and mindless, refusing to acknowledge God or deal with God is losing out. They've lost touch with reality because they lost touch with God himself. I have a lot of friends who were very close to me when I was living in a different area of the country and I keep touch loosely through text messages and phone calls but the truth is that we have lost touch; we have lost the touch of truly knowing one another in an intimate and deep way because we don't spend time together. We may chat once a year and talk about things in our lives but we don't really know each other intimately. This is what happens in our moment when we begin to look at our circumstances in our life and equate it to what's going on around us. We've lost touch with who God is, and what God is able to do. When we lose touch with God, we become mindless and empty, following the crowd instead of realizing who He is and being able to be intimate with Him and His authority in assurance, knowing that He wishes to grant whatever that we ask because we are His and He loves us and wants to help us. It is so easy for us to get bogged down by our situations, our world, the microcosm of things that we deal with on a daily basis.

But if we would truly embrace who He is and quit losing touch with that reality, then our whole worldview would change. Who is God? Do you doubt his ability or do you doubt His "want to"? Are you stuck looking at the waves and the situation surrounding you and you've lost touch with who He is? Quit focusing on the waters and focus on the Wave Walker. He is so much more than our finite mind can ever understand. If only we would stay in touch with Him in an intimate way, then we know that because He can, He will.

But you, dear friends, carefully build yourselves up in this most holy faith by praying in the Holy Spirit, staying right at the center of God's love, keeping your arms open and outstretched, ready for the mercy of our Master, Jesus Christ. This is the unending life, the real life!

Jude 1: 20-21

BUILD UP!

I woke up this morning to a fire being built by my husband so he could sit outside on a cold morning and enjoy the beauty of the outdoors. He carefully chose the right size kindling and wood, centering it all in the firepit and building it up from the bottom. Then the fire had the right amount of oxygen and fuel so that it could become a powerful source of light and heat. God wants us all to be powerful sources of His light and warm the world around us with His love. He has given us the tools, the fuel and the Spirit to build up ourselves in the most holy faith. He has provided the instruction to keep ourselves in the center of His love with our arms open and outstretched in anticipation of His mercy. But we often forget to light the fire. We have all the materials but we must have the spark. We must take the tools and use the kindling around us to build ourselves up. If we just sit like a lump in our disappointments, the fire has no oxygen and cannot catch hold. If we refuse to build ourselves up in His grace and mercy, it is like lighting a fire with no wood to burn, our hope fizzles a minute and goes out. The real life, the unending life like a fire takes a constant source and balance of fuel and oxygen. This means we need to constantly stay in His word, in prayer and in praise so that we are building up ourselves in the faith through the trials. This is so that the fire of God reigns in our lives instead of false fires or passions of worldly means. Jude says "carefully" build. Carefully means full of care. Care is serious attention or consideration to doing it correctly so no harm is done. Carefully building up in the faith means through scripture and prayer not through tearing others down. Taking fuel from another person's fire so you can build your own doesn't make Your fire. When a burning log is removed from the others and set alone, it soon burns out. This is why we are encouraged in scriptures to bind together in faith with other believers so that our source remains hot and connected. Let the fire of God be built in your life. Quit allowing the dampening and darkness of the circumstances around you to quench the Spirit who gives you the oxygen you need to harness the fire of faith. Praise through your storms.

Praise sets faith fires aflame.

Is there anyplace I can go to avoid your
Spirit? to be out of your sight?
If I climb to the sky, you're there!
If I go underground, you're there!
If I flew on morning's wings
to the far western horizon,
You'd find me in a minute—
you're already there waiting!
Then I said to myself,
"Oh, he even sees me in the dark!
At night I'm immersed in the light!"
It's a fact: darkness isn't dark to you;
night and day, darkness and light, they're
all the same to you.

Psalms 139: 7-12

Morning's Wings!

I admit that I love a lazy morning where you can watch the dawn and know you are not under pressure to be somewhere or do something in the next hour. As I sit here in the quiet of the morning with the pitter patter of rain falling and the warmth of the fire, I truly feel the blessings of God surround me like a warm hug. Psalms 139 is a song of hope, deliverance and encouragement that rings through my morning. It is so refreshing to know that God is everywhere at all times. David reminds us that God is there in the highs and lows of life. He is there in the good and the bad, the light and the dark. I love this picture of the eagle in Alaska. We went out in a boat to go whale watching and saw an incredible amount of eagles. They are so majestic and huge. I could only imagine soaring away on their wings to the far horizons but even then knowing God was there. In fact, God doesn't depend on light to see us or know us. He doesn't need us to say a word to know what we are thinking as He knows but He still cares enough to take the time to hear a child pray. He knows the intimate details of our thoughts but still finds the time to listen to us whine, rant and rave all in anticipation of that moment when we realize that no matter what, He is there. I often disappoint myself that I cannot be in multiple places at once. I cannot do everything I would like to do or be all the things I would like to be but I can be what He wants me to be…just me. I often feel like I am not enough or not good enough but then I remember who I am in Him. When I feel unseen and hurt that others fail me, I can remember who He is and that no matter what He is there before me waiting on me. He sees me even in the dark…in fact, He is the light in the darkness and there is never a place too dark that He cannot be seen. In my darkest moments, He is there with me as my light and He sees me as clearly as if it was daylight. So here is the question…why would we want to avoid God's Spirit or to be out of His sight? It will never happen but why would we want that? Sin. Betrayal. Deceit. Lies. Falseness. All these things of darkness try to obscure the truth of who He is and yet…He is there patiently waiting for us to see the Light in our darkest places. When we run from who He is into our own place of defeat, we find ourselves in a dark cave of oppression and defeat…then suddenly in the midst of the darkness, the light flickers and we see Him. We can choose at that moment to sit in our place of misery or we can climb out to the Light.

I can't believe how you waver—how easily you have turned traitor to him who called you by the grace of Christ by embracing an alternative message! It is not a minor variation, you know; it is completely other, an alien message, a no-message, a lie about God. Those who are provoking this agitation among you are turning the Message of Christ on its head. Let me be blunt: If one of us—even if an angel from heaven!—were to preach something other than what we preached originally, let him be cursed. I said it once; I'll say it again: If anyone, regardless of reputation or credentials, preaches something other than what you received originally, let him be cursed.

Galatians 1: 6-9

PROVOKED AGITATION!

Not too long ago, we had to replace our washing machine and the previous machine didn't have an agitator so we opted to get one that did this time as we knew it was an important part of the process. Sure enough, clothes that had previously gone dingy began to brighten again and the awful smell from "clean" clothes was now not an issue. I had really liked the other machine because it was a deep, large machine that could hold large loads but I was deceived by the size thinking less loads was better. Don't think we walked around with smelly belly clothes for years...it wasn't that at all. It was the "level of clean". The truth about each of us is this: some of us are happy with being somewhat clean and a little dirty when it comes to sin. Sin is sin. You can color it in pretty colors and call it by different names but it doesn't change what it is to God. The only persons who are fooled are those who fool themselves because the Spirit of God is witness to this and is a con-victing spirit. An agitated person is a person who is mixed up and confused about the truth. In Galatians, Paul writes that there are false doctrines and teachings which agitate and confuse Christians into accepting lies as truth. It doesn't matter what their credentials are, if they speak contrary to God's word or thwart it to make it fit their doctrine, then it isn't of God. An agitation can be a good thing when it is surrounded by Living Water for the water will wash the filth away that is stirred up by the agitator. However, if you get into a situation where you are not full of Living Water but running a little dry, the agitation can confuse and further ingrain falseness, lies, deceit and the other dirt of sin. Let me speak clearly! Sin brought into the church under the guise of political correctness is still sin no matter what it is called. Alternative messages like alternative lifestyles are not of God. This is why our world is so confused. They come to the church for Living Water and receive stale, dirty sewage watered down from politicians and policies that are not of God. Whether the message be "name it, claim it" or alternative lifestyles in the pulpit, both are lies and not of God. They are completely alien, not minor variations. Paul states that they are cursed when they stagnate the word of God with lies. We cannot take a false doc-trine, dress it up and call it God's word without consequences. God's word has purpose. It is quick, powerful and cutting. It sears up from wrong and steers us to right. It isn't about feeling good in our sinful lifestyle but more about separating from the sin. Recently I was in a situation where the sin around me was rampant and tangible to the point that just looking at it seared my eyes and caused tears. I immediately wanted out of the venue but was stuck for a while as I attempted to exit and although the decor was astonishing and the glitz/glamor superb...the sin made all of it look dirty to me as clothes covered in sewage while the agitator washed the sin further and further into the threads. So much of our world today is sewage threatening to wash into the threads of our lives because we stay in the muck rather than standing in the shower of Living Water. The devil goes about as a roaring lion seeking whom he may devour. We need to be cautious and careful about where we go, who we associate with and we need to carry the instant shower of His word for circumstances that seem like truth but are really just traitorous filth that will cause us to waver. If it causes you to question your salvation or your faith, take it to Jesus to be washed. Lies and deceit are in every hand. Walk wisely, full of his Spirit so you can evade the wiles and traps of Satan. Greater is He that is in us than he that is of this world.

Mortals make elaborate plans,
but God has the last word.
Humans are satisfied with
whatever looks good;
God probes for what is good.
Put God in charge of your work,
then what you've planned will take place.

When God approves of your life,
even your enemies will
end up shaking your hand.
Far better to be right and poor
than to be wrong and rich.
We plan the way we want to live,
but only God makes us able to live it.

Proverbs 16: 1-3, 7-9

Elaborate Plans!

Motives. The hidden agenda. The reason. God knows them. Committed to God, our plans are His and He makes them work according to His will and timing. Boy, do we often wish we could control that timing from birth to death but if we commit it to Him and leave it there, He will make it as it should be and in our favor. The issue is that we are often like a child who makes a plan that isn't feasible because of an outside force or circumstance they are not familiar with, that only their parents can see. We try to steer them carefully so they won't fail but often they refuse to listen or acknowledge our guidance, so their plans fail or turn out disappointing because they failed to do as we instructed. I remember my boys building their legos & tinker toys like Lincoln Logs and I would listen to their plans and think to make that work, you are going to need to change your plan. Sometimes, they would ask for my help but quickly, they would get through the current issue then refuse further help as they wanted to do it their way. This is so us with God. We say we give it all to Him and to His leading but the truth is that we only want Him to correct our errors then let us continue on our path. We think our plans are better. It feels impossible to wait on an unseen hand to direct our future when it is so easy to do it ourselves. I used to make cakes for weddings and events. There is a lot of work, time, planning and effort that goes into one cake. As the cake was built up, it required stabilizers to keep it from falling completely apart during assembly. All the pieces had to be placed with exactness and one small wobble could collapse the whole. I don't do cakes anymore or rarely, not much since my kids were young because I found others who can create my ideas without the stress involved on my side. I know what they have to do to make it work but I trust their mastery of their skill. The plans we make fall into the realm of the Masterplan created by the Master Creator. Only He is able to bring our plans to fruition in His timing and His ways. When God approves of your life, even your enemies will sit back and applaud because they are impressed. Quit settling for only what looks good instead of what is good for He has purpose for your life. It is far better to struggle financially and be in His will than to be rich and out of it. All your wealth and fame amounts to nothing if God doesn't approve. God is our parent who patiently watches us plan and implement but He sees our errors, successes and ways ahead. He often steers us into a better way and when we ask, He corrects our erroneous ways but it is up to us to include Him. His plans are higher and wiser. He sees the Masterplan. He can choose to allow us our own way or deflection can happen. He is not subject to our whims and wills unless He chooses to be subject to them. He does hear us and when we align our ways into His, there is peace in knowing that the Master will take care of it and you need not worry. God sees our hearts. He sees our hidden agendas and our motives. He knows us better than we know ourselves. Perhaps trusting in the Mastermind who is creating the Masterpiece is a better decision than going it alone.

Let love be without dissimulation. Abhor that which is evil; cleave to that which is good. Be kindly affectioned one to another with brotherly love; in honour preferring one another;

Romans 12: 9-10

DISSIMULATION!

I am a million dollar word girl as I read a lot but I was unsure about the meaning of this word in context so I had to research it. Dissimulation in pure meaning is without concealment or pretense. Dissimulating is an act of faking an emotion. Fakes or falseness in relationships are soon found out when hard times hit. This is why "falling in love" is such a dangerous concept. Truth is I never fell in love with anyone; I chose to love them. Oh yes, there was infatuation and lust and puppy dog feelings but those quickly fade when bad habits or irritations occur. Love without falseness means to love without thinking of yourself. It means being willing to sacrifice your happiness for the other person's dreams and finding your happiness in the togetherness. If both people in that relationship are willing to do this, there is nothing to stop that kind of love because it is without boundaries. God's love is like that to us. He went all the way to death for us before we even existed. There is no hiding of anything in God's love. Darkness hides things. Evil obscures things. But love conceals nothing. It reveals the truth of itself through kindness and honor. Honor is a noun meaning high respect or regard, placing another higher than oneself in esteem. Preferring one another with kind affection means that love is demonstrated as an act of selfless sacrifice. Loving God means it isn't about you but about trusting who He is and that He has as much desire for your happiness as you do. Recently I had to make a very hard choice in love. I had to choose to love through an impossible situation. That means choosing to love the other person no matter the cost to yourself. I will not lie to you; this kind of love takes practice. When we first "fall in" love, it is an emotion of attachment and attraction but it has no foundation yet. The foundation of true love is established by choices and building life together whether that be by parent/child, marriage, friendship or even in spiritual connections. God's love is deep and wide because He chose us before the foundations of the world. Imagine a God who knew people would act so badly and hatefully towards Him but yet He loved so deeply that He willingly accepted death on a cross to spare these people from a fate worse than death-a fate He prepared for Satan himself and his minions. Imagine this God looking down at mankind emulating Satan as a worthy being to worship on the altars of our lives, sacrificing our children to this beast who had despised God himself and yet...knowing this...Jesus willingly laid down His life in love. What love. I had a really low point a year or so ago where I had literally soiled myself in the hospital and all of those around me who were supposedly caring for me left me in that condition sitting in a wheelchair in my own mire. I couldn't do anything about it because I couldn't help myself as I had just had back surgery. I will never forget the love and attention of my husband as he tenderly cared for me and cleaned me up and brought me back to myself. I had hit the lowest point in my life and he tenderly loved me back through his tender care. He didn't ask a nurse or anyone else to help. My mother was there and assisted him but he was the one who sacrificially ministered to me. That was love. That was honor and kind affection with no falseness. Love isn't an emotion that comes and goes. Love is a choice. God chose to love us and we are instructed to choose to love without pretense, ulterior motive, or falseness. We are instructed to abhor evil and cleave to good. Today is a day that the world celebrates love as a yearly holiday. For me, it is also a day of celebration as our wedding anniversary is tomorrow. But such love as what God has demonstrated is much deeper than an ocean, more vast than the horizon and just as overwhelming. God loves you unfathomably. Choose life in Him. Choose His love. Choose.

**Investigate my life, O God,
find out everything about me;
Cross-examine and test me,
get a clear picture of
what I'm about;
See for yourself whether I've
done anything wrong–
then guide me on the road to
eternal life.**

Psalms 139: 23-24

THE UNCLOUDED DAY!

I woke up this morning after a very rough night following one of the toughest days of my life. As I walked outdoors to let the dog out, I couldn't see, for the fog settling heavily on the ground. The sound of the coyotes was loud and the feeling of dread tried to lay upon my spirit and heart until I looked at the road and yard reflecting the water standing in the potholes and sinkholes. As I looked over to them, I saw the moonlight refract on them and heard God whisper in my mind and heart that He knows where the potholes are in my life and I can trust Him. Life is real through heartache and loss. Life is hard to walk but God knows the road ahead. He knows there are deep ruts and hard places to walk through the heavily clouded and foggy days but He also is the guiding light in those places. It is simply a matter of trust. When our hearts are broken by misplaced trust or grief or betrayals or other things, God is the peace-speaker. We have a choice. We can trust His guiding hand even through the dark, hard places or we can go it alone risking the road to destruction. Mindset is the challenge. We can choose to see the ways ahead as part of our journey trusted into His keeping and choose to see the fogginess as moisture sent to embrace us and water us or we can see it as a deterrent to the path, stagnating us from moving forward, leaving us stuck in a rut we cannot get out of and whining, complaining and moaning about how unhappy we are. It is a choice. Each moment of each day is a choice to hold onto Him on this rocky road of life even though we don't understand or we can choose to do it our way. I have always been a forward looking person even through my toughest parts of the journey. I will admit that the road yesterday had a lot of pitfalls but I also have to tell you how God told me ahead of time. On Sunday, He gave me a word that I felt was for one particular family but turns out it was for me too. He told me that there were a lot of boulders in the road ahead, rocks that may seem insurmountable, but there was a choice to fall upon them in anger and frustration or to pick them up and build an altar with them. Jacob wrestled with God on one of his toughest nights. He was forever injured from that night with a limp in his hip from the battle scar but he chose to pick up the rocks and build an altar to God on that road that changed him forever. His name was changed by God to Israel and his legacy is enormous. He had been a deceitful thief who came to a place of reckoning with God. God embraced him, changed him and called him by a new name. I don't know your journey or your way ahead but I do know God and He is trustworthy. He is the God of the unclouded day, where there is no night nor grief. He has promised us this in His word and He is trustworthy. Time to rest in Him for the journey ahead is rocky and fraught but He is the light in the foggy night and His road leads to eternal life. He sees me. The deepest parts of me. He gets a clear picture of me as He tests me and tries me. Then He guides me in the ways of righteousness. Investigate my life God. Know me. I trust you.

"Set up signposts to mark your trip home.
Get a good map.
Study the road conditions.
The road out is the road back.
Come back, dear virgin Israel,
come back to your hometowns.
How long will you flit here
and there, indecisive?
How long before you make
up your fickle mind?
God will create a new thing in this land:
A transformed woman will embrace the
transforming God!"
I'll refresh tired bodies;
I'll restore tired souls.

Jeremiah 31: 21-22, 25

REFRESHED AND RESTORED!

Bone tired and bone weary are phrases used to illustrate extreme fatigue. Fatigue comes from overdoing what your body can handle and pushing past your limits. God says He will refresh tired bodies and restore tired souls by transforming us when we embrace this transformative God. Recently I have traveled a bit and slept in different beds, gone to meetings and pushed myself to my limit and beyond. I have felt bone weary in my body and exhausted in my energy stores. Emotionally I have stretched to the max and needed refreshment so I understand the need for rest, refreshing and restoration. Here in Jeremiah, God poses a question to us. How long will we flit here and there, indecisive, trying to make up our fickle minds about who God is and what He will do? God is ready to create a new thing and transform us but we must first set our mind on Him and home. As we travel, I notice things along the road such as mile markers, sites I recognize and sadly, I notice crosses of remembrance. When we hike, I make note of the way in and the way back because I am not great with directions and can easily get lost. This is what God is saying in this verse. Set up signposts of remembrance for the travels of life. Get a good map and study the trails in advance, understanding the conditions so you are prepared for the trip before you go. Plan it out and mark it so that when you are bone weary and travel tired, you can easily see your way home to the place of rest and refreshment. Sometimes we are forced on journeys not of our own making through this life especially when Someone else takes the lead and we are in for the ride because of choices they've made but we are bound to them emotionally or physically. This is the time to begin to make signposts and study the road conditions in depth to escape the mire. Many good people have gotten trapped in snares set by Satan because of side trips they took with their spouses or children or other loved ones without studying the road conditions in advance. Many times the road back changed and became impassable due to unforeseen things but God sent and prepared a way through the impossible. Grief is one journey that often leads us into a bone weary travel without a way back unless we study the road in advance and put down markers for that journey. I have watched and grieved with so many in the last couple of years from unexpected deaths of children to cancer related deaths to age expected but still painful losses. In each instance, there was a journey through grief that is painful and difficult and different for each person. Some have grieved silently and others loudly; some have grieved through signposts of memories and others through celebrations of life. Grief is a journey of soul weariness and bone deep but God gives us a good map in His word and tells us to come home to rest from our grief. There is a way back. There is light again, love again and joy again. There is a trip home but the journey must be taken. God will create a new thing. God will transform us when we embrace Him. Grief doesn't come just from the loss of a person. It also comes from loss of a life desired, a dream, a relationship, a marriage, a way of life, a home, a job, and many other things. Grief is a journey of change and comes in many ways. Whatever journey of grief you have taken, for whatever reason, there is a way home and transformation to joy. The road out to where you are is the way back. Call out. He will hear you and make the signs clear. Come home.

My counsel is this: Live freely, animated and motivated by God's Spirit. Then you won't feed the compulsions of selfishness. For there is a root of sinful self-interest in us that is at odds with a free spirit, just as the free spirit is incompatible with selfishness. These two ways of life are contrary to each other, so that you cannot live at times one way and at times another way according to how you feel on any given day. Why don't you choose to be led by the Spirit and so escape the erratic compulsions of a law-dominated existence? * * * Galatians 5:16-18

ANIMATED & MOTIVATED!

This picture of a tree with odd growths and things looks fully animated like it is a cartoon character trying to talk and yet I know that these odd growths are a result of unfortunate and unforeseen things occurring to the tree that were not supposed to happen. In Galatians, Paul contrasts the spirit of freedom with the spirit of selfishness. Self indulgent thought and jealousy or envy of others is a trap of slavery. The root of sinful self interest is at odds with a free spirit-they are completely incompatible. We cannot go from slavery to selfishness and back to freedom of spirit without complete repentance. The root has to be dug out so it cannot feed the compulsions of selfishness. We cannot live with selfishness at our core and live freely because God's love isn't about selfishness but about self sacrifice. When life is about me and my wants and my needs and my desires and my dreams and me, my, mine...it is rooted in self or flesh. Love unlike lust is not rooted in flesh or selfish desires but rather all about constancy. If we live day by day by how we feel or our emotions, we live in an erratic place of inconsistency as our emotions are volatile and can be changed. We can choose to be led by God's spirit and in that we have complete confidence. Confidence in who we are is found in consistency and truth. If someone is constantly supporting and loving us despite our emotions and our willy nilly ways, we feel confident in their love and it transfers to our spirit. If we are constantly demeaned and put down then we have no confidence in love. Selfishness and love cannot coexist. Law is left to interpretation and often is led aside by emotions and political persuasion or passions but God's love is completely without the root of selfish desire. A tree grows as it is set. When something happens to it, it continues to grow as best it can despite the circumstances, around the disease or hurt or harm to reconstruct itself based on the root of what it is. It continues to produce fruit, seed and grow as long as it has itself rooted. I have watched trees completely cut off to stump and they regrow because they are still rooted. Examine your roots. Where are you rooted? Selfish desires Or love? Self-interest or self-sacrifice? Our lives will grow from where we root. We can grow through the pains of life into fulfillment despite the pains. Recently I watched a film that told how the burl or deformation can make the tree itself more valuable in certain situations just like the pains of life and growth experiences give us great value to others. We become not because we are but because we learned through the hurts and pains. Our legacy is not because of ease but because of trial. Our testimony comes because of the test. It is a choice. Happiness is a choice. Love is a choice. Freedom is a choice. And none of these are free. Why don't we choose to be led by the Spirit of God instead of the erratic compulsions of selfishness? It is our choice. I think this tree chose to live through freedom and so it is free and animated, motivated by its roots to be who God desired it to be. I choose to be a tree planted by Living Water so my roots grow deep in His love and no matter what comes my way, I will grow through it to become what He designed me to be.

A white-tailed deer drinks from the creek;
I want to drink God, deep drafts of God.
I'm thirsty for God-alive. I wonder, "Will I ever make it–
arrive and drink in God's presence? "I'm on a diet of tears–
tears for breakfast, tears for supper.
All day long people knock at my door, Pestering, "Where is this God of yours?"
These are the things I go over and over, emptying out the pockets of my life.
I was always at the head of the worshiping crowd,
right out in front, Leading them all, eager to arrive and worship,
Shouting praises, singing thanksgiving–celebrating, all of us, God's feast!
Why are you down in the dumps, dear soul? Why are you crying the blues?
Fix my eyes on God–soon I'll be praising again.
He puts a smile on my face. He's my God.
When my soul is in the dumps, I rehearse
everything I know of you, From Jordan depths to Hermon heights,
including Mount Mizar. Chaos calls to chaos, to the tune of whitewater rapids.
Your breaking surf, your thundering breakers
crash and crush me. Then God promises to love me all day,
sing songs all through the night! My life is God's prayer.
Sometimes I ask God, my rock-solid God, "Why did you let me down?
Why am I walking around in tears, harassed by enemies?"
They're out for the kill, these tormentors with their obscenities,
Taunting day after day, "Where is this God of yours?"
Why are you down in the dumps, dear soul?
Why are you crying the blues? Fix my eyes on God–
soon I'll be praising again. He puts a smile on my face.
He's my God.

Psalms 42: 1-11

DEEP DRAFTS!

Thirst is not just a physical longing or need but also an emotional and spiritual one. As David penned this song, he was comparing the physical need of thirst in a deer to the need for satiation of spiritual and emotional solace from God. He asks "Will I ever make it-arrive and drink in God's presence?" At this point, he is very down in the dumps and frustrated with life. He feels bereft and let down as he runs for his life. He is so confused because he is a worshiper and a friend of God but at the moment, he cannot seem to find solace in God nor answers. Everyone around him is saying "where is your God?" As in, things don't look so good for you and you trust this mythical God so why? David's heart is yearning for God. Yes, He wants God to step out and show up big, resolving all His problems in wonders but mostly he yearns for the place of peace and contentment in the midst of his storm. Let me assure you that he finds it and God was always there. He just got his eyes off God and onto his circumstances which led him to a place of thirst-running, panting and longing. I know about thirst in the body and how dehydration affects you mentally, physically and emotionally just like drying up from God's living water is like a grape becoming a prune. Dehydration from lack of spiritual water is more dangerous to the body than physical dehydration. Recently we struggled with hydration of the cells in my mom's body via chemotherapeutic means. She would come each week after chemo to receive a bag or two of rehydration fluids full of vitamins because cellular death of the good cells was happening along with the bad due to the chemo. We found all kinds of supplements and tried many ways to get her to drink because it was necessary for her health. When you don't feel good, nothing tastes good so it was very hard. Finally, with God's help, we were able to get things moving in the right direction and she began to be thirsty and drink. This is the thing for us to grasp--the key to revival and renewal isn't the right song, message, preacher, setting, etc. but rather a thirst for His Living Waters above all else. Much is said about revival but true revival is when all else fades in light of the thirst for His presence. David reveals his whole journey in the song. He was focused on his situation and began to thirst for God as he moved away from Him into his own devices, running for his life. He talked the talk and said the right things but now he says he is on a diet of tears meaning he has cried, pleaded and begged God but then he finally begins to really reflect and remember what God had done in His life and his groveling and pity turned into worshiping and counting His blessings. When he began to remember the God feats and the feast of provisions in God's stores and fix His eyes on God instead of the current, the chaos of the whitewater rapids became a song of God's power and might. He begins to refresh himself in God's glory, and drink in His promises. As he delights himself in God, he saturates his soul in His presence and once again begins to see God for who He is instead of wondering where God was...the water doesn't leave the source...the person wanders away from the source. Why are you down in the dumps, dear soul? Why are you crying the blues? Fix your eyes on God and not the circumstances and soon you'll be up praising again. Rehydration doesn't take place immediately. It is a process of continuous refueling and cleansing. It takes a while for starved cells to come alive again. Revival comes because we hunger and thirst for Him above all else. Cellular restoration comes because we thirst for Him constantly and not just desperately. An IV weekly at church on Sunday only gets you so far...cells that lack hydration take more than an occasional flood. They need a steady flow of His living water. Take a deep draft, a big gulping drink of water then see how long until you are thirsty again. Our spiritual need for Him is real. Yes, we need two big gulping drafts once in a while but we need His steady flow through us and in us to truly experience soul regenerating revival. Lacking energy, feeling stale and stuck, begin to praise; draw nearer to where the flow is and begin to drink in His presence. Soon, you can say like David and I - He puts a smile on my face. He is my God. No other can fill me like He does.

I'm glad in God, far happier than you would ever guess— happy that you're again showing such strong concern for me. Not that you ever quit praying and thinking about me. You just had no chance to show it. Actually, I don't have a sense of needing anything personally. I've learned by now to be quite content whatever my circumstances. I'm just as happy with little as with much, with much as with little. I've found the recipe for being happy whether full or hungry, hands full or hands empty. Whatever I have, wherever I am, I can make it through anything in the One who makes me who I am. I don't mean that your help didn't mean a lot to me—it did. It was a beautiful thing that you came alongside me in my troubles.
Philippians 4:10-14

The Secret to Happiness!

Everyone wants the secret recipe to happiness for it drives the industry of our world. "Have it your way" has been the prevailing thought which has raised a very spoiled generation of people who are disconnected and discontented with everything and everyone. Paul shares the secret recipe to happiness in Philippians openly. Learning the lesson that whatever we have and wherever we are, we can make it through. Christ Jesus is the answer to the true definition of happiness. Happiness is an emotion that we have been sold as a product to believe that we have to have it. Actually the freedom to experience happiness is more a state of mind that comes from recognizing who we are in Christ Jesus. Need and want have become confused in our world by many who feel discontent because their wants are not immediately met. A baby who has a wet diaper is discontent because after a bit it becomes uncomfortable. It doesn't matter that he was the one who caused it…he cannot resolve the situation on his own so he begins to cry out. If left in that situation, the baby would eventually get a nasty rash that will turn into an infection that could be very serious. This is an example of need because he cannot truly change the situation on his own without help. We as a blessed people rarely have needs that we cannot reach out to another to meet but we have a need for a Savior. We have created a dirty diaper of sin in our lives that must receive His changing power to rid us of our own situation that we caused. He has already paid that price and stands ready to hold us, comfort us, change us, keep us fresh and growing in Him. But many of us refuse to get past the complaints and whining diaper state of development. We actually know and have been trained to walk in faith into a place of quiet contentment and understanding of happiness but we are so busy playing we get distracted and wet our diaper rather than taking care of the Matter. Then we begin to whine and complain that it didn't go our way and demand a diaper change again. Contentment in Christ Jesus is the answer to happiness. Realizing that we have everything we need, no matter what in God, is the Secret to happiness. Happiness is knowing the Savior and living life in His favor. Making a change in our behavior to accommodate the truth of contentment is the secret. I love this picture of the sun shining directly on the flower though the flower's face is turned away. It reminds me that if we bloom where we are planted and when He decides then His Son-shine is in our soul and we can demonstrate joy in Jesus as His reflection spreads happiness through us to those around us just by being. It is a choice.

Choose Happiness.

Friend, don't go along with evil. Model the good. The person who does good does God's work. The person who does evil falsifies God, doesn't know the first thing about God.

3 John 1:11

THE MODEL!

In 2nd and 3rd John, there is only one chapter each and when reading these personal letters, one can question why they were included as part of the holy scriptures because they really don't have a lot of content. I have pondered them a lot and wondered. Then a revival broke out on a college campus. Suddenly the news was amazing about what God was doing by some and contrary by others. Now I understood why these letters were included. These letters are addressed to certain individuals and talk about other individuals in warning. The crux is this verse in 3rd John 1:11. Model the good. It is not our role to decide whether God is or is not moving in a particular person or ministry but rather it is our role to model good which is to uplift anything done in the name of Jesus that aligns with His word. John says, "Friend, don't go along with evil. Model the good." He is instructing us and the early church to be who God intended us to be. Be the difference. A sum is two or more added together. It is so easy when one person begins to complain to jump on the bandwagon and join them because we truly all have complaints about things. I mean why not? The reason why not, is here! Model the good. I was speaking with a loved one recently about their role in life and they had had a hard time with something. I asked them if they had looked at it differently. Being the difference means not subtracting from the good but being what remains when all the naysayers take away from the total. Yes, your job may be tough, your spouse may be slacking, your finances may look bleak and your day may start off bad but you still have the opportunity to be the difference. What does that mean? It means that when all the others are taking away from the job through complaining, you can be the difference in counting the good. It means when you find lack in your spouse, your kids, your life...you pick up the slack by counting their positives. It means when things look bleak and times are hard, you share with others the meager benefits you have. It means while others are doing evil and falsifying what God is doing, not knowing the first thing about who God is, you be the difference and be The Good. Notice it doesn't say Be Good. It says Be The Good...the difference. The other day, I set aside some broth in the fridge and noticed the next morning how it had separated in the fridge. The thick fats had risen to the top like cream does and then the bone broth settled to the bottom rich in minerals and vitamins. It was a visual difference. Be The Good means to be The Visible Difference in life. Be the one who brings sunshine to the journey of life. Be the one who counts the clouds and therefore sees the rainbow before anyone else. Be the one who challenges the status quo by rising to the challenges of life from marriage to career by being the visionary and the servant of God. Count The Good. Be the Good. Model The Good. We are God's own children here but for a moment. Time is the one quality in life that we can never get back so use each second to reach out a helping hand. We have so much to give so give it. We are so blessed, so bless others. Bless from your lack. Share what you have with those who have not. The person who does good, does God's work. That is all He has called us to do. Don't take away. Don't tear down. There are plenty of people who will. Be the difference who still stands when the others have taken away. Be the difference who builds back the sum total and more because you stood in the gap. Don't go along with the evil detractors. Be The Good.

Soak me in your laundry and I'll come out clean, scrub me and I'll have a snow-white life. Tune me in to foot-tapping songs, set these once-broken bones to dancing. Don't look too close for blemishes, give me a clean bill of health. God, make a fresh start in me,
shape a Genesis week from the chaos of my life.
Don't throw me out with the trash, or fail to breathe holiness in me.
Bring me back from gray exile,
put a fresh wind in my sails!
Give me a job teaching rebels your ways
so the lost can find their way home.
Commute my death sentence, God, my salvation God, and I'll sing anthems to your life-giving ways.
Unbutton my lips, dear God;
I'll let loose with your praise.

Psalms 51: 7-15

SOAKED LAUNDRY!

I love paper-white flowers otherwise known as narcissus papyraceus. They are a sign of spring and fresh life after winter. A Genesis week or beginning again from the dead to life. David writes this song to God in a place of repentance. He longs to start again and feel the freshness of God's anointing upon him but he also realizes that God knows all his flaws and sees him as he is. He says he's been in gray exile. I have some laundry in gray exile too. It needs a good bleach soaking to take away the minerals and grunge that has built up. I have watched people take their towels and soak them, being surprised that they come cleaner than out of the washing machine and I understand the truth which is the difference in soaking and washing. Washing is often not thorough enough when the gray of life has soaked deeply into our souls. The deposits of grunge and gray have built up over time and turned our once white clothes into a beige or gray. This is when it is time for a good soak...not a quick wash but a long soak and scrub to break down the good that has become discolored and tainted. This is when you look and decide is it worth salvaging? Of course it is, says God. He can still clean us up and make us like new by a deep soaking wash and cleansing of His Holiness. It starts with our willingness to endure and walk out the soaking. Soaking isn't a quick process and it isn't always easy on the fabric but it is necessary to see the vibrant colors and the true whites. It requires us to tune into Him and His ways and to tune out the ways of man to sacrifice our agenda for His and our plans for His and our comfort for His provision. Freshness! Sweetness! Life! Beauty and Holiness all come from soaking in His presence. We cannot soak if we are distracted by the everyday pressing in and we cannot soak if we are in a hurry worrying about what's next. Soaking through to holiness requires preparation and willingness to yield. My yard gets soaked after a good rain when it cannot contain any more water and it begins to run off taking minerals and dirt away with it leaving behind that which was rooted deep. This kind of soaking is when the presence of God is profound and deep but comes mightily breaking out and sparking revivals but the soaking to Holiness requires sacrifice of time, comfort and willingness to let everything take a back seat to what God is doing because with the soaking comes the scrubbing. Without the scrubbing, we are wet in His presence and some of the loose debris has broken loose but the deep-set things that have built up are still set in the fabric of our lives. Only through a thorough scrubbing can these things be broken loose and cleansed away to true snow white Holiness. God is preparing His people. He says if it can be shaken, it will be shaken as He prepares the scrubbing of our lives so our garments can be made ready to be His bride. No blemishes left, no tatters or tears, no deep seated and hidden agendas, nothing but Him left. We must yield to this soaking and scrubbing in order to be His bride. It isn't about MardiGras or Ash Wednesday. It isn't about Lent or putting away in fasting. It is about soaking in His presence and allowing the essence of who He is to permeate us so deeply that it breaks loose those things that have set in us for far too long preventing us from being who He desires us to be. It is about the scrubbing of the things in our lives that prevent us from being fully yielded as we give up the hold onto these things that we cherished with all our effort and all our desire. It is completely allowing Him to bleach out the deep dark stains of built up hurt, anger, resentment and bitterness that have rooted and hidden deeply in our spirits spoiling our fabric into a dingy color without our awareness. Cleanse us deeply God! Soak us and scrub us into Your holiness.

Change your life, not just your clothes. Come back to God, your God. And here's why: God is kind and merciful. He takes a deep breath, puts up with a lot, This most patient God, extravagant in love, always ready to cancel catastrophe. Who knows? Maybe he'll do it now, maybe he'll turn around and show pity. Maybe, when all's said and done, there'll be blessings full and robust for your God! *

Joel 2:13-14

ALL'S SAID AND DONE!

I am always amazed at the amount of laundry we have from clothing changes throughout the day. We start our day early and so many times my husband has done three different types of things from running errands to outdoor tasks before I am barely moving. When I began to read in Joel today, this jumped out to me. God wants us to make change to us, not just the clothes. God is kind and merciful in every situation. He probably often has to take a deep breath to handle some of mine that I get into...requiring a lot of patience and loving perspective. In this chapter, Joel is prophesying the end of days that are approaching quickly. He is telling all the terrible things that will be occurring then he calls out a charge to repentance in verse 12 followed by these verses. Why do we change our clothes? To be fresh, to do different activities, to be prepared, because a certain venue requires certain clothes? When do we change our lives? Moving? Marriage? Death? Divorce? What Joel is saying here is that God is saying Enough is enough! It is time to change...not to just move or down-size or get somewhere different but to truly change deep in our heart. Not a temporary measure like a clothing change where it lasts for a few hours, days, weeks or even a few years but a full change...a complete 180 towards God instead of the worldly focus we have had. Quit looking ahead to what might be in our earthly walk to what will be in our eternity. Catastrophic things are about to happen that will astound and terrify the world. But God who controls all circumstances says that He is in control and only He can cancel the catastrophes ahead if we fall on our faces in repentance. Maybe He will stop the hurricane, the tornado, the wars, the famines, the disease and pestilence. Who knows but God? Even now the pouring out of His presence upon the Earth is coming to pass as foretold in this passage of scripture thousands of years ago. This tree has clung to this side of the mountain for hundreds of years, growing and curving into itself to strengthen its grip. It clings to life rooted but growing. If that tree had not changed its natural tendency to grow straight and tall, it would not be there today because it would've fallen into the ocean below. The tree had to make a core change and root deep in order to sustain through life. We need to turn back to God and each time our natural tendency to wander and grow away comes about, we must redirect ourselves back into His presence. We cannot just change a solitary moment but rather we must change our mindset, our focus, our very being into the design of who He rooted us to be. When all is said and done-when the world is come to that place of no more-when this existence becomes untenable, we will step into His presence full of robust blessings for God who saved us from all the chaos because we turned back to Him. The time is now. It is time to change, to reverse course and turn towards the God of the impossible and the God of the possible. He can still turn things around for us and we shall see that He truly is Good.

Do two people walk hand in hand if they aren't going to the same place? Does a lion roar in the forest if there's no carcass to devour? Does a young lion growl with pleasure if he hasn't caught his supper? Does a bird fall to the ground if it hasn't been hit with a stone? Does a trap spring shut if nothing trips it? When the alarm goes off in the city, aren't people alarmed? And when disaster strikes the city, doesn't God stand behind it? The fact is, God, the Master, does nothing without first telling his prophets the whole story. The lion has roared— who isn't frightened? God has spoken— what prophet can keep quiet? * * *
Amos 3:3-8

QUESTIONS??

Signs of the times are everywhere and questions fill the hearts of all of us about timing and life in general. Amos was a prophet of God who knew God's voice intimately and he knew God was faithful to reveal Himself through His prophets firstly then through signs. Amos poised rhetorical questions here because they make us think. This picture is a photo of yet another river that has turned blood red in Russia this time. These end time signs are examples of what things will be like when Jesus returns for His bride except now these rivers are poisoned with metals and chemical runoff that is killing crops and animals. The metal smells like blood but is explained away scientifically just as the Rapture of the church will catch so many unaware and be explained away. There are trumpet sounds being heard in the air across several countries being explained away and flying objects in the air being explained away...all preparations for the great deception by the Antichrist who will lie, deceive and call himself god. Notice the first 5 questions are all answered with a no and then the two that follow are answered yes. The Lion of Judah has roared notifying His prophets that judgment is nigh and His prophets cannot keep quiet for they are called to sound the alarm that disaster is about to strike and the trap is going to be sprung. The innocent will be felled and the two walking hand in hand will be separated if they are not on the same path to Heaven. The time has come. I will be very frank. I have struggled with this message most of the night last night and throughout the day today because it isn't an easy message. God, the Master, is prophetically dishing out the words and news of His imminent return. The signs and wonders surround us and yet are being ignored and blamed away, pushed aside and plundered for deception. The world is groaning with earthquakes and tsunamis as well as many other natural wonders for all of nature hears and recognizes that the Creator is fed up with His creation and is coming soon to met out fierce judgment upon this people. The alarm is sounding and yet so many are caught up in their own agenda that they refuse to tune in. They have heard the message so often that they have grown immune to the urgency. I beg you to please hear me. God is speaking and saying that He is coming for His bride who has taken the time to prepare, watch and pray with trimmed wicks lit awaiting His arrival. If you have grown cold, old, stale or not refueled, I beg of you to do so now. This vision He has shared over and over with me through the years is becoming clearer and more refined. The day and hour are drawing near. The Lion's roar still echoes through the night as His return happens.

Woe to you who turn justice to vinegar and stomp righteousness into the mud. Do you realize where you are? You're in a cosmos star-flung with constellations by God, A world God wakes up each morning and puts to bed each night. God dips water from the ocean and gives the land a drink. God, God-revealed, does all this. And he can destroy it as easily as make it. He can turn this vast wonder into total waste. Seek good and not evil— and live! You talk about God, the God-of-the-Angel-Armies, being your best friend. Well, live like it, and maybe it will happen. "I can't stand your religious meetings. I'm fed up with your conferences and conventions. I want nothing to do with your religion projects, your pretentious slogans and goals. I'm sick of your fund-raising schemes, your public relations and image making. I've had all I can take of your noisy ego-music. When was the last time you sang to me? Do you know what I want? I want justice—oceans of it. I want fairness—rivers of it. That's what I want. That's all I want.
Amos 5:7-9, 14, 21-24

FAR FLUNG!

This background photo is of the oldest tree known to man. Nicknamed Methuselah for the oldest man who ever lived. I just imagine all the things this tree has seen as time has pushed past and around it. Each morning God wakes this world of ours and puts it to bed at night but He never sleeps because He is not in need of that. He does rest though as stated in Genesis. God rested or paused when He saw that what He had made was good. We like to say that God is our best friend but do we live like it? What does God want from us? He desires justice and fairness through worship. Here is an honest question: when is the last time you sang to God of your own volition without an agenda or being prompted at church? When is the last time you spent time focused only on Him? Friendship with Jesus that is only one sided isn't fair or just. Calling upon Him in our needs but not taking the time to say thank you and spend time just for Him is like always being the friend who takes but never gives. That kind of relationship destroys friendships because the person fatigues at always being taken advantage of and never given into. Amos says "Woe to you who are always full of vinegar through your trampling of God's word and time." God is tolerant and good but there is a limit to what He will take when His righteousness is constantly stomped into the mud. He can take the vast wonders of this Earth and turn them into wastelands with a word just as He created them with one word. He desires for us to seek good and not serve evil. He doesn't want shows, conventions and agendas. He wants us in conversation and time spent. My youngest son had a favorite book as a child called The Giving Tree. The story of the tree is an allegory to what Christ gave. It is a story of a beautiful tree that started life with a child who spent time climbing and playing in friendly conversation with the tree but as he grew, he changed to becoming a user. He was given the blessings of the fruit from the tree to sell to provide for himself and his family but soon that was not enough. Then the very life of fruitfulness was given by the tree as the boy took the branches. Next the whole trunk was cut down as the tree sacrificed its own self for the boy's happiness and yet still the boy went his own way ungrateful and unaware by choice of the sacrificial part. As he approached the end of his own life, the man now had used up all of the tree and finally returns to the stump as the place to rest, the headstone of the grave with the realization that the tree had been there all the time-the boy had failed to realize the things that mattered until the end of his own journey. God is calling to us to turn back and realize who He is and give Him the whole of who we are in glory and honor before the close of time. Methuselah lived almost 1000 years. The namesake tree has lived much longer than that. God, the creator of both, has no beginning and no ending. He is our friend. Isn't it time we realized and set aside time just for Him? Not time to be caught up in our day nor time that is spent in a corporate worship though that is important also. What God deserves and desires is friendship time. Time where we recognize who He is and just walk in the garden with Him in the cool of the morning or evening or all day. If God is truly your BFF, then take measure of the time you are spending with Him and readjust your expectations. This Wonderful God desires oceans of His love to be poured upon you and He deserves the oceans of justice in our time to acknowledge who He is.

"Oh yes, Judgment Day is coming!"
These are the words of my Master God.
"I'll send a famine
through the whole country.
It won't be food or water
that's lacking, but my Word.
People will drift from one end of the
country to the other,
roam to the north, wander to the east.
They'll go anywhere, listen to anyone,
hoping to hear God's Word—but they
won't hear it.

Amos 8: 11-12

WORD HUNGRY!

We take so many things for granted and one of those is the word of God. We go from place to place, season to season without valuing the one thing we have grown so used to having access to but not using fully. I have a special place where I keep recipes from my mom and grandma because I value them. I will pass these down to my own family in the future. God's word is a valuable asset that most have a copy of in their home like the recipes of the best dishes but often both of these are seldom used and rarely observed. God's word is the recipe to a successful life and a vibrant future that we should walk in and use daily but sadly, most of the time, it is set aside and rarely opened. This is why when the deceiver comes as the antichrist, he will deceive many. It is easier for someone to deceive when the truth isn't known. In a day and age when technology has ownership of so much, many rely on the Bible apps and such to procure the word of God but when reliance on these becomes complete, the word can be altered and changed into what man wants. Just look at examples of history. History is being rewritten before our very eyes and even some who lived through it begin to question their own memories. Stories passed down generation to generation change until they no longer have veracity. I remember the story of a young woman cooking a roast and she cut the corners off before putting it into the pan. When asked by her new husband why she did that, she responded because my mom did. Then they called her mom and asked her why...and she responded because my mom always did that. They then called the grandmother, who laughed loudly, because she had always cut the corners off because her pan was small. Judgment day is coming and even now is here without us realizing that it has come. God's word has been changed and thrashed, manipulated and tainted. Celebrities and TV preachers have taken God's holy word and changed it to fit their desired outcomes pushing it into the mainstream as His word when it has been taken from context and changed. His word warns us not to do this and that the famine of truth will spread through the whole country. It isn't a famine of food and water but something more essential. It is a famine of truth. The famine is spreading and the gospel of truth has been taken and changed. Please listen to what I am saying. We need to get an older Bible and begin to commit the words to our hearts because the days of hidden messages and deception are upon us. The gospel of truth even now is being hidden and the judgment of famine from His word is approaching us on every hand. Listen and learn. Read and store up His words in your heart. People even now are wandering church to church to hear the truth but it has been so tainted that it is hard to find. Hide His words in your heart so you might not sin against Him and so you can hold onto it until the end.

My Master, God-of-the-Angel-Armies,
touches the earth, a mere touch,
and it trembles.
The whole world goes into mourning.
Earth swells like the Nile at flood stage;
then the water subsides, like
the great Nile of Egypt.
God builds his palace—towers soaring
high in the skies,
foundations set on the rock-firm earth.
He calls ocean waters and they come,
then he ladles them out on the earth.
God, your God, does all this.

Amos 9: 5-6

A MERE TOUCH!

My world has been shaken lately with the mere fragility of the human body. I have lost many friends in the past few weeks to unseen and sudden things which are unexpected and my world has trembled and gone into mourning. God thankfully has not trembled nor fallen. He continues to see value in me as He builds His palace towers. God isn't caught off guard by the things that cause me to tremble. His touch on the earth causes earthquakes and tsunamis to form because the very minerals recognize the touch of the Creator. My boys laugh at my sweet puppy because he trembles in excitement when I am near and especially when I am about to sit down because he knows that he gets to be with me. I imagine this is how the Earth and all creation feels towards God as I know I do. I tremble in anticipation and excitement of His presence daily even though I know He is always there. It is an excitement in me to see what God is doing or about to do across the land, in our lives and in the world. When the boys were little and thunder roared, it made them fearful until I explained that it was God bowling the lightning strike across the sky. It was the sound of lightning as it sparked and sizzled sent by a mighty hand of God. Why is that less frightening? Because of trust. We see the natural occurrences of nature play out on a world stage but those who trust in God have no fear for we know these are but trembles in anticipation of His presence. We can science it up all we want but the truth is that God is in control and at one word the storms brew or cease. The Earth trembles and rolls in anticipation of the day He will step foot out of the clouds. What a day that will be! When the queen of England was in her castle, and I am sure it is the same for her son who is now king, there was a flag that was mounted on the top of the building stating that she/he is in residence there. Joy is my flag that I wave high in the castle of my heart for The King is in residence there! God, our God does all this...the wonders, the joys, the floods and tides...His presence is life.

Jonah was furious. He lost his temper. He yelled at God, "God! I knew it–when I was back home, I knew this was going to happen! That's why I ran off to Tarshish! I knew you were sheer grace and mercy, not easily angered, rich in love, and ready at the drop of a hat to turn your plans of punishment into a program of forgiveness!

Jonah 4: 1-2

I KNEW IT!

In reading the book of Jonah today, I was caught by how anger ruled Jonah's life and yet God used Him. Jonah was furious many times in this book and yet he did not repent of his anger. He used his anger as a weapon to keep himself from God's calling but God taught him a lesson of great magnitude in the belly of the fish. But his anger, he kept with him and God continued to deal with him in spite of it. I know some angry people as they sit in judgment of others, some furious at God and some furious at life. They know that God is sheer grace and mercy, not easily angered and rich in love. They know he is all about forgiveness and they count on it for themselves as they allow their anger to rule their lives but oh how furious they get when things don't go their way. Just like Jonah. In Matthew, when Jesus speaks to the Pharisees, He uses the phrase Jonah-evidence to indicate the absence of proof. He alludes to the story of Jonah in the whale as the 3 days that Jesus Himself would be gone and then goes on to address forgiveness and attitude. Why is this important? Because we get angry at God for being God. We charge ahead wanting all that is good for ourselves but not wanting God's favor and forgiveness for others. We go through the motions of life wanting good for us but angry when the tree of promise for us withers even though God was the one who brought the tree for cover anyway. I honestly do not know what happened to Jonah but I hope he finally found repentance and redemption from his anger because I see how it held him back from enjoying the wealth of God's goodness and blessings. Anger is an emotion and not a fruit of the Spirit. Anger works negatively in our lives and can lead to a loss of all that God has given us because we are not content with who He is even when we know that is who He is. He knew it. He knew God would forgive and save with mercy and grace so he ran to prevent God from doing what God does but he learned that God is God and that made Him furious. He lost his temper and yelled at God. What a sad day it is when we cannot celebrate the goodness that God does in someone's life. What a sad day it is when we allow anger to steal our joy. God brought up a tree overnight to bless Jonah and he enjoyed the blessing but then when a worm ate the tree, he got angry again not realizing that God was trying to show him the pattern of what anger was doing in his life. Allowing anger to rule you eats away the good things that God provides for you. Be very careful. Anger ruling life is not of God. Jonah says I knew it-you are not easily angered. There is such a thing as righteous anger but it is tempered with forgiveness and mercy. Don't be a Jonah. Don't lose out on the blessings because of your anger and sulking. Allow God to be God. He has good things for you. Ask for forgiveness and walk in His mercy. Rejoice for those who succeed around you and delight in His blessings. He has good things for you but temper towards Him is not the way. What is your Jonah issue that is holding you back from being all that God desires for you? Are you struggling with anger at God for not giving you the child, spouse, job, career or other that you desire? Are you angry because you feel He blesses others and not you? Are you frustrated and howling because He hasn't healed or performed the miracle you wanted for yourself or your family member? You know who He is. He is God. He is blessing you and loving you in His way and in His plan. Embrace who He is instead of howling in anger like a toddler not getting her way. He wants good things for you but you refuse to see them and acknowledge them because you want something else. Stop, look and listen before you end up like Jonah.

"God's Judgment Day is near for all the godless nations. As you have done, it will be done to you. What you did will boomerang back and hit your own head. Just as you partied on my holy mountain, all the godless nations will drink God's wrath. They'll drink and drink and drink— they'll drink themselves to death. But not so on Mount Zion—there's respite there! a safe and holy place! The family of Jacob will take back their possessions from those who took them from them. That's when the family of Jacob will catch fire, the family of Joseph become fierce flame, while the family of Esau will be straw. Esau will go up in flames, nothing left of Esau but a pile of ashes." God said it, and it is so. * * *
Obadiah 1:15-18

BOOMERANG FIRE!

The beauty of the rainbow is undisputed but the fullness of it is rarely seen except from an airplane because we are looking up not through. Songs have been written about, over the rainbow, myths spun about riches and pots of gold and the truth remains that the rainbow reminds us of promise no matter how much others try to taint it with other meanings. The rainbow is a symbol of God's promise that on judgment day He will not flood the Earth again. No, this time the Earth will be judged with unquenchable fire. What is it about Esau? He seemed like a decent guy, forgiving and mature. Yea, he made a foolish decision but why does it matter? Esau is a symbol of all who despise the promises of God. Esau sold his birthright, his blessings from God for a bowl of soup. He gave up all that God had planned for him for a portion of self indulgence without a thought. It is crazy to think that God preferred a lying, sniveling, cheating sneak over a man who wanted to work, hunt and do. An honest guy who just was hungry and didn't understand the value of what he was selling lost out on all of God's promises because of a careless moment. Scripture quotes God as saying Jacob, have I loved, but Esau I have hated. I never want to be hated by God so what must I do to make sure that I am never in that place? God is love. The rejection of His blessings and His love by Esau; the very flippant way he cast off God's gift as of no importance, of less value than a common meal was the beginning of his trouble. Esau's family becomes a nation called Edom who to this day still harasses Israel. Wanderers and nomads willing to sell out family for their own gain is what God despises. People who are not fixed in His promises but will sell their soul for fame or fortune get God's wrath. Understand this: God's promises are not for sale. The only access to His fullness is by complete acceptance of who He is. A boomerang is a tool that is sent out with the intention of it returning with its purpose achieved. God says what you do and have done will boomerang back to you. If you mock God, God will mock you. If you are godless, despising His values, His wrath will be dished upon you. But those who anchor in Mount Zion-the love of God-will be safe, protected by His promises. God's judgment day is near. Safety and rest are had only to those who dwell within his shelter of promises which can only be obtained by walking in His love. "Somewhere over the rainbow" missed the mark. It is through the rainbow of God's loving promises that we find sanctuary. Jesus was willing to give all so you could walk through the rainbow of love into the fullness of His promises but you must yield your desires to Him. Quit holding onto the anger, frustration, fear and disappointment. Let your bitterness and hurt go. Give it all to Jesus. Jesus is coming again very soon.

You who sit down in the High God's presence,
spend the night in Shaddai's shadow,
Say this: "God, you're my refuge.
I trust in you and I'm safe!"
That's right—he rescues you from hidden traps,
shields you from deadly hazards.
His huge outstretched arms protect you—
under them you're perfectly safe;
his arms fend off all harm.
Fear nothing—not wild wolves in the night,
not flying arrows in the day,
Not disease that prowls through the darkness,
not disaster that erupts at high noon.
Even though others succumb all around,
drop like flies right and left,
no harm will even graze you.
You'll stand untouched, watch it all from a distance,
watch the wicked turn into corpses.
Yes, because God's your refuge,
the High God your very own home,
Evil can't get close to you,
harm can't get through the door.
He ordered his angels
to guard you wherever you go.
If you stumble, they'll catch you;
their job is to keep you from falling.
You'll walk unharmed among lions and snakes,
and kick young lions and serpents from the path.

Psalms 91: 1-13

DECLARING VICTORY!

Wow! Tough night as I wrestled with truths I didn't want to face last night. This verse is God's word and He says Fear Nothing! Those are strong words. As I let my puppy out to potty, I could hear the coyotes and I thought what fear that their cry invokes in us. Declarations of victory do not come without battles but they do come before the battle, during the battle and after the battle meaning they are a constant. Say this-God, you are my refuge and I trust in you and I am safe! Say it again and again. He rescues us from hidden traps and shields us from our own foolishness. His huge outstretched arms protect us and fend off all harm. We are safe in his shelter. He says Fear NOTHING! Not wild wolves at night nor flying arrows in day, not disease nor disaster even if you see others dropping from these things. How hard it is to stand in this and be still when we see the arrows headed our way and the fear rolls towards us but we must snuggle into His place of refuge knowing that He has it all. I would love to say we can depend on others but the truth is that many times the failure of systems and people let us down which often turns us fearful and distrusting towards a God who hasn't failed us. Where we go wrong is when we walk out of the refuge into the battlefield without our armor. We forget that He has provided us the tools of victory and we strut out from His protection into places we are not armored to handle because we failed to gear up and prepare before the day of battle began. Then we come running back cowering in defeat rather than gearing up. It is time we go to the enemies' camp and take back what was stolen from us as we fought unprepared. We need to soak in His power and might, gear up and get busy fighting instead of living in defeat and cowering in mistrust. God doesn't give us a spirit of fear and defeat but of love and a sound mind. We need to know who the truth is in and quit walking around in defeat wondering if. Is God able? Is He willing? Is He on time? The answer to all of these is yes, even when you feel the weights of life surround you. So how? Say this-God, you are my refuge and I trust in you and I am safe! Say it again and again. This is where we get our armor! Begin to say it and believe it while you praise and uplift.

On your feet, Daughter of Zion! Be threshed of chaff, be refined of dross. I'm remaking you into a people invincible, into God's juggernaut to crush the godless peoples. You'll bring their plunder as holy offerings to God, their wealth to the Master of the earth.
Micah 4:13

JUGGERNAUT!

All of the signs are here and those who specialize in weather are shouting it out through video, social media and other sources that today is headed to be a very dangerous day. The winds have already started blowing and are supposedly scaled to be extremely high all day. Things look bleak, but God. As I listen to the weather authorities telling me to prepare by getting all the loose things that can fly around put up, I am reminded that these are unusual circumstances and they are trying to help us prepare. The Word of God is full of weather reports and warnings to us of what is to come and be, telling us how to prepare and yet many of us move along in our lives as if things are unchanging and not attuned. In Micah 4, the report is to clear the external and worthless things out of our lives so that our true selves can be molded into God's image and design. Micah is the weather prophet foretelling the coming of the refinement through storms and challenges. He tells us to get the loose and worthless out of our lives so we can focus on who God is as He remakes us into an invincible juggernaut. I will admit this is not a word I use much nor hear often but it means a force to be reckoned with that is superior in all ways-the best of the best of the best. As the weather spills out the warnings for today, I am reminded that God has been sending us messages telling us to prepare for a while. We are a stubborn people who have not listened but the weather report is more urgent. The tornado of God's wrath is headed this way and His return to catch His bride away is imminent. He wants us to clear all the loose and useless in our lives so that He can refine us into the invincible juggernaut He wants us to be, to withstand the forces that are coming our way. Then as we stand in His might, He gives us the autonomy and authority to bring the plunder as holy offerings to Him. He wants us to stand in all authenticity and authority as an invincible force against the tide of evil and He will do the crushing and remaking into the persons He desires us to be. Holy offerings of wealth will be brought unto God as we experience His gifts and His power. The power of the wind is something that fascinates us all because we cannot tame it from hurricanes to tornadoes to just blowing winds, it remakes our world in an instant with incredible force. Grab this! That untamable force of wind is from the same breath of God that He breathed into us. We are an untamable and unstoppable force of God when we allow Him to work through us in His mighty way. We are more than we think or comprehend when we yield ourselves to the Master of the Wind. In His hands, we are mighty forces of unexplainable change and juggernauts of faith that stand through the strongest onslaughts of hell. We may not want the storms of life to come but they come to clear us of the chaff-the outer coverings that prevent us from becoming fruit and the remaking into steel and iron of a juggernaut only comes when all the impure dross of useless things are removed from our lives. God wants His breath to blow pure, holy and forcefully into the lives of those around us prepared for the storms, withstanding the onslaught. He is calling us to prepare ourselves. The weather warnings are out. Time to take action!

Then he told them what they could expect for themselves: "Anyone who intends to come with me has to let me lead. You're not in the driver's seat—I am. Don't run from suffering; embrace it. Follow me and I'll show you how. Self-help is no help at all. Self-sacrifice is the way, my way, to finding yourself, your true self. What good would it do to get everything you want and lose you, the real you? If any of you is embarrassed with me and the way I'm leading you, know that the Son of Man will be far more embarrassed with you when he arrives in all his splendor in company with the Father and the holy angels. This isn't, you realize, pie in the sky by and by. Some who have taken their stand right here are going to see it happen, see with their own eyes the kingdom of God."

Luke 9: 23-27

DEAD END!

What an adventure the last 24 hours have been! God has been so faithful in ways we cannot imagine. I have learned over the last few days to Thank God as He truly is in the driver's seat. It's really easy to want to give up sometimes and drop our hands in frustration and walk away from our situations. But God has infinite purpose in what He has given us and tasked us to do even when we get tired and fatigued. We try to live in the world philosophy of self; we want everything we want, when we want it and we often get ourselves in really bad situations, some of our own making and some that are outside of our control. Yesterday, a tornado literally formed in the back of my learning center yard and we watched it form through the window. As we grabbed the kids and ran to safety in the interior part of the building, sheltering in place, telling them to be careful and that God was with us, inside we couldn't help but quake because we know how nature is fickle and things happen. But I wanna testify That it was like the very hand of God sat down upon our building. Everyone calmed even while lights were exploding, and building sounds were swishing and groaning...it was terrifying, but God. He was there in the midst of the whole situation and He kept us. We can look at the damage today and we can realize that we were in a precarious situation. We can see how His hand performed a true miracle yesterday for us. Why is it, that in the moment, it is so hard to trust? Often our situation seems like it is a dead end with a tornado surrounding us as in the picture and we cannot move, and our hearts are struck with complete fear. It is at these moments that we must realize the same God, who was in the driver's seat at the moment of a situation we couldn't control is in the driver's seat in all situations. Pie in the sky by and by is a phrase indicating a hopeful position of future dreams. When Luke says this is that, he is stating that this is a realized expectation not a fake possibility or prediction. We had no warning yesterday on our phones or radar of that tornado. It simply dropped suddenly and unexpectedly. This is how situations occur and we are often unprepared but God knew that tornado before and placed His hand on my center and all within it. God knows before we do and He has prepared a way. There is no sense in having shame about anything. He has prepared us for what He calls us to do because He looks forward to His time with you. He isn't embarrassed of you. He loves you with everlasting love. He is trustworthy. Embrace what He has brought you to and trust Him. He is a confident and knowledgeable driver.

The purged and select company of Jacob will be like an island in the sea of peoples.
They'll be like dew from God, like summer showers
Not mentioned in the weather forecast,
not subject to calculation or control.

Micah 5: 7

PURGED AND SELECTED!

It is on my bucket list to view the northern lights in person. The Aurora Borealis fascinates mankind with the beautiful display of light which is really akin to lightning in its magnitude and structure. The lights are really the very violent and powerful reaction to energized particles from the sun as they slam into Earth's atmosphere at speeds of up to 45 million mph but the God created magnetic field protects us from the onslaught by redirecting the particles toward the poles (there are southern lights too). The lights cannot be predicted, controlled nor can the colors be directed except by God. These tremendous demonstrations of His handiwork are on display all the time but we are only aware of them when we direct our attention towards them and what they are. The magnificence of these lights is overwhelming and powerful but it is really a display of a purging and selection process of our atmosphere set in motion by God Himself. We must travel to different areas of the globe to see these electrical storms in action as they are not visible everywhere due to the redirection of the protective magnetic field He created. We can only wonder what they are except when storms of lightning come our way.

Purging and selecting is a very violent and harsh process because it requires ridding ourselves of things that make us less than what we are supposed to be. When God purges us, the process isn't very fun but it is necessary to help us become the select company of His delight: the unique island in the sea of people. The people of God are compared to dew from God not something forecast by man, controlled by man, mentioned by man or subject to man. The people of God are a force directed by only God Himself. I heard and read a story recently about a lady praying for a need to be met loudly and repeatedly outside as she worked. Her neighbor wasn't a believer, treated her unkindly often and one day decided to teach her a lesson. He purchased the items she had been praying for and put them on her porch, rang her doorbell and hid. As she saw the items, she began to thank God loudly and profusely. Immediately he popped up and said she was fooled as it wasn't God doing that but him. Then she began to thank God even more because now she knew that God had used the bad in her life to produce good. The fact is that we are all subject to Him and Him alone. We can choose to be a tool of His hand and rejoice when He uses circumstances to bless or teach us or we can choose to ignore His hand moving and say it is circumstance. Our choice of how we see it doesn't change what it is. The aurora borealis is a magnetic storm of violence visible to our eyes as a thing of beauty. We can choose to see the things in our lives as storms of violence or auroras. It is all perspective. Some days all we see are lightning strikes, hear the thunder and feel the ripping of the tornadoes while in others we see the aurora. God is calling us to allow Him to be our magnetic shield from the onslaught of evil so that the redirection and reflection of the storms in our lives can be beautiful auroras others can see rather than the tearing down. God let us be surrounded by the magnetic field of Your glory so that when the onslaught of energized particles of evil impact our lives, they are redirected and reframed into Your Aurora of beauty, grace and love. Let us be northern lights that guide and direct Your presence while shining beautifully and reflecting Your glory in the midst of our storms of life.

But he's already made it plain how to live, what to do, what God is looking for in men and women. It's quite simple: Do what is fair and just to your neighbor, be compassionate and loyal in your love, And don't take yourself too seriously— take God seriously. Attention! God calls out to the city! If you know what's good for you, you'll listen. So listen, all of you! This is serious business. * * * Micah 6:8-9

ATTENTION!

What is God looking for in men and women?

Simple. People who take God seriously and themselves lightly but are fair and just neighbors who are compassionate and loyal to all around them. He has made it plain that He has our lives in His control. All we must do is honor Him with all of us. Let's look at it one piece at a time. Taking God seriously means that He has full control. Yesterday we got a new puppy and boy was his attention challenged as we showed him the great outdoors. As he learned the appropriate places he could and could not go, he kept returning to this statue to try to get into its lap. He had already discovered that the lap of a person is soft and rewarding. He was so confused exploring this statue. It wasn't a real lap and didn't have all the things he was looking for. When God calls for our attention to take Him seriously, this means He wants us to tune in and listen. To do so means we must put aside those things that distract us from the purpose and plan He has for us. There are lots of shiny distracting fake laps out there that say and look like places to shelter, refuge, take rest and anchor but on closer observation, they are much like this concrete statue was to our puppy…unbending and unwieldy. Fair and just, compassionate and loyal are traits that Micah uses to describe the kind of person God wants us to be. Fairness has been taken out of context in our society to mean all equal and that isn't the true definition. Fairness is treating others as they deserve to be treated. It is being impartial while delivering just treatment without favoritism. My students would complain "that isn't fair" sometimes when one student received an unexpected but deserved reward and I would explain to them that "life isn't fair" but God is and I am. Each person is rewarded but it isn't the same for all. God doesn't have favorites that he treats better than others. He is just as He directed us to also be. Just means holding to a standard of accountability. To be just right, it has to meet a standard of measurement. In calling us to be just and fair with compassion and love, God is calling us to demonstrate His love felt through His eyes and heart, according to His laws and standards. He wants us to not throw His love out lavishly and foolishly to those who will ignore it but rather look on those who need and desire to be loved, then to love them deeply and wholly.

But me, I'm not giving up. I'm sticking around to see what God will do. I'm waiting for God to make things right. I'm counting on God to listen to me.
Micah 7:7

COUNTING ON GOD!

This photo looks like a bunch of water flowing through a small area of outlet under a natural bridge but in reality, it is a closeup photo of a hole in a shingle in the roof of my building after a tornado threw something through it. The reality isn't always what we picture it to be in life. Often we look at a situation and think it is one thing when it is really another. As I taught the children yesterday in Kids' church, I overheard a conversation that struck me as the perception of kids' is vastly different than ours. The kids were discussing what thunder really is. One kid told another that thunder is God dumping potatoes out while the other kid argued that potatoes are under the ground and not in the sky. It was hilarious listening to them as they negotiated the terms of belief about what thunder is. I could just imagine God shaking His head and laughingly looking at us in the same manner in which I looked at these kids, as we negotiate the beliefs we cling to in our world. In a day and age where reality is often lost in misconceptions, we are instructed to stick around to see what God is doing, wait on Him to make things right and count on God to really hear and listen to us. Our world is fraught with tricks of mind, slight of hand and mischievous lies as truth is spun and torn. This is why God gives us these instructions because at first glance we are easily misled. This is why He tells us to hide His words in our hearts, so we might not sin against Him. God knows the intricacies and details of our situations and has already planned a way of escape or refreshment. He knows the goings on, going in and going out of our lives. He has placed promises in His word for us to anchor to, count on and stick with, no matter what comes our way. In the book of Micah, this prophet saw all that was going on but determined in his heart to count on God. This is our path. No matter what it looks like, remember that the reality is likely not what it looks like and trust God.

God is good,
a hiding place in tough times.
He recognizes and welcomes
anyone looking for help,
No matter how desperate the trouble.
But cozy islands of escape
He wipes right off the map.
No one gets away from God.
Why waste time conniving against God?
He's putting an end
to all such scheming.
For troublemakers, no second chances.
Like a pile of dry brush,
Soaked in oil,
they'll go up in flames.

Nahum 1: 7-10

DESPERATE TROUBLE!

Who do we rely on during the impossible? This is our refuge. No matter how desperate our situation, God is still God. Yesterday I had a conversation with a bird. It was a little one-sided as he was super busy flitting and eating berries in the bush outside my patio door. The bush literally teemed with birds eating. They are a special type of bird called a cedar waxwing and evidently a big deal to get to see. I saw hundreds literally in my backyard traveling as a flock, they discovered the berries and had a blast eating and communicating with one another. I asked the bird how it is that he so easily relies on what he cannot see, has no idea about tomorrow and just trusts that provision would come. He didn't answer me audibly of course or I might be in a hospital somewhere but God spoke clearly His words into my heart where I had hidden them. No eye can see, no ear can hear, nor can we even imagine what God has prepared for us. This is 1 Corinthians 2:9. It is a refuge promise. When life becomes seemingly impossible and harder than you think or believe, He will make a way through that impossibility. No matter how desperate it looks, God is always there ready to be our help in tough times and our hiding place through our troubles. No one escapes from God. People can try to hide behind their cloaks of evil where they invoke harsh times upon God's people but He sees all and He is done with all the lies and schemes. He will take the troublemakers and turn their schemes into kindling soaked with their oily evil and He will light the flame. These birds traveled from place to place trusting that God had provisions for them. They had no idea I had just remarked a few days ago how the berry bushes had really produced an extra large amount of berries this year. But God knew. His way of provisioning isn't our way. We are walking into a deeper place of trust in Him which requires us to walk boldly and confidently knowing that He is our provider, our source and our way. He has set the path of victory and provision in front of us. We just need to take wing in His wind and trust His direction. The old song says, "I care not today what tomorrow, if shadow Or sunshine or rain...The Lord I know rules over everything and all of my worry is vain". Is this the time we are desperate for Him?

What's God going to say to my questions?
I'm braced for the worst.
I'll climb to the lookout tower and scan the horizon.
I'll wait to see what God says,
how he'll answer my complaint.

Full of Self, but Soul-Empty

And then God answered: "Write this.
Write what you see.
Write it out in big block letters
so that it can be read on the run.
This vision-message is a witness
pointing to what's coming.
It aches for the coming—it can hardly wait!
And it doesn't lie.
If it seems slow in coming, wait.
It's on its way. It will come right on time.

Habakkuk 2: 1-3

WRITE THIS!

Ever wondered why something happened or why God allowed it? If not, you are not human. It is a human trait that we question why. In life, there are so many things that don't go how we would like them to go from health to wealth to all of it! Habakkuk had the same thing. He had a list of complaints of how some people were getting it all and others were getting unfair amounts of bad things. What's God going to say to our questions? He answered Habakkuk by giving him a vision and told him to write what he saw.

I wait to see what God will say to my complaint and He says Write this! The answer is coming! It is on its way. If it seems slow in coming, just wait...it is worth the wait. It will come right on time. Time change is coming this weekend and it always messes everything up for a few weeks until our bodies adjust just like when someone who is on a night shift moves to a day shift. Our schedules get all convoluted. Our time is not always the same as everyone else. I know my mom and I discuss how others in our lives don't have the same sense of urgency about things as we do and we sometimes find that frustration gets to us. I think we transfer some of our frustrations to God when things we think should happen in a certain time/way tend to get off kilter and put off. Habakkuk said he was braced for the worst but planned to climb to the lookout tower and scan the horizon for the answer from God. And God gave him a vision to be written out for us to read. The thing that I embrace most from this text is that God answered his complaints with a vision of hope for the future. God heard his cry and his frustrations and his irritations. God listening is a major thing to celebrate but God acting is mind boggling. God not only heard and listened but responded with a vision of the future and gave instructions for Habakkuk to write it out so it could be read on the run or in a hurry. Here's the message so you can write it on your mirror in lipstick or on your fridge or post in your car... wherever you are so you can see it and read it on the run. Are you ready? God doesn't lie. This is a message of what is coming.

Write this! God is an On Time God. This is the definition of life.
Read it. "Look at that man, bloated by self-importance— full of himself but soul-empty. But the person in right standing before God through loyal and steady believing is fully alive, really alive."
Habakkuk 2:4 MSG
I don't always understand His plan nor His ways but I do trust His hand and His heart. So what is God going to say to my questions and complaints? Write this! The answer is on its way and it will be on time. Trust God!

Though the cherry trees don't blossom
and the strawberries don't ripen,
Though the apples are worm-eaten
and the wheat fields stunted,
Though the sheep pens are sheepless
and the cattle barns empty,
I'm singing joyful praise to God.
I'm turning cartwheels of joy to
my Savior God.
Counting on God's Rule to prevail,
I take heart and gain strength.
I run like a deer.
I feel like I'm king of the mountain!

Habakkuk 3: 17-19

King of the Mountain!

King of the Mountain is a child's game that is very fierce and competitive because there can only be one. As a child, everyone wanted to win because we didn't realize that King of the Mountain comes with mountains of responsibilities and to be King of the Mountain, you must fight through the hard times to get there and continue to fight to stay there. I still remember us playing this on the trampoline as our mountain. The goal was to be the first one up and you had to keep bouncing. If anyone made you fall, you toppled off the mountain to start all over again with the new king. The feeling of winning is very addictive and enticing but the constant stress and pressure of remaining King eventually wore us down until we gave up or quit. This verse in Habakkuk puts it all in perspective. It's not about us. See, we spend so much time competing to be what we already are through Jesus. There is only one King of all the mountains of life but He has conquered all so we can reign with Him in eternity without the stress. Yes, we still may battle in this life through temptation and trials but if we remember that the battle is already won then we can rejoice in that! We can thrive knowing that even if life gives only lemons, He has made them full of the juice and sweetness to make lemonade. Even if things don't go as we want and desire them to go, He has already gone before us to the place of victory and laid out the path in front of us. He isn't the king who kicks us off the mountaintop to battle it out again and again but He has shown us favor and invites us to share in His win. He invites us to His table of feasting and celebrating. He invites us to turn cartwheels of joy in the middle of our struggle knowing that He has the Rule to prevail through all our troubles. Habakkuk had it right when he said that we can take heart and gain strength, run like the deer and sing joyful praises because no matter what the circumstances, God is king of the mountains and has conquered them all, inviting us to rule in elation with Him. Winning builds confidence and when we walk tall in confidence, it is attractive to those around us. It draws others to Him. No matter what the mountain is that we are trying to conquer from health to wealth to self to hell, Jesus is the king over all. Even if it all looks impossible, He still holds His hand out to boost us up to the mountain to reign with Him. Though the fruit fail to blossom and ripen or even if they are full of worms and rot in the fields; though the checking account runs dry and the cash seems tight, the future looks bleak and the days are long...sing joyful praise because it isn't us that reigns alone responsible for the mountains. He is King and we are His people. Those barns that are empty are because He has prepared us a feast. Those fields and opportunities that are stopped short are because He has a better opportunity for us. Those trees and investments that aren't profitable or productive as they should be are still rooting and growing deeper in Him. It's not about us. It is about Him. Start praising Him in the Even If and watch change happen. The King of Glory will arise in Praise and He will hear our cry and lift us from the miry pit onto the top of the mountain to reign with Him! The God of the Mountain is still God in the valleys. When things go wrong, He will make them right. He's God in the good and the bad. God of the day is still God at night. Remember who the King of the Mountain is and rejoice in Him! Let's lift up our hands and let Him reach down to lift us up!

"Quiet now! Reverent silence before me, God, the Master!
Time's up. My Judgment Day is near:
The Holy Day is all set, the invited guests made holy.
On the Holy Day, God's Judgment Day, I will punish the leaders and the royal sons;
I will punish those who dress up like foreign priests and priestesses,
Who introduce pagan prayers and practices; And I'll punish all who import pagan superstitions
that turn holy places into hellholes. Judgment Day!" God's Decree!
"Cries of panic from the city's Fish Gate, Cries of terror from the city's Second Quarter,
sounds of great crashing from the hills! Wail, you shopkeepers on Market Street!
Moneymaking has had its day. The god Money is dead.
On Judgment Day, I'll search through every closet and alley in Jerusalem.
I'll find and punish those who are sitting it out, fat and lazy,
amusing themselves and taking it easy, Who think, 'God doesn't do anything, good or bad.
He isn't involved, so neither are we.' But just wait.
They'll lose everything they have,
money and house and land. They'll build a house and never move in.
They'll plant vineyards and never taste the wine.
A Day of Darkness at Noon
"The Great Judgment Day of God is almost here. It's countdown time: . . . seven, six, five, four . . .
Bitter and noisy cries on my Judgment Day, even strong men screaming for help.
Judgment Day is payday—my anger paid out: a day of distress and anguish,
a day of catastrophic doom, a day of darkness at noon,
a day of black storm clouds,
a day of bloodcurdling war cries,
as forts are assaulted, as defenses are smashed.
I'll make things so bad they won't know what hit them.
They'll walk around groping like the blind.
They've sinned against God!
Their blood will be poured out like old dishwater,
their guts shoveled into slop buckets. Don't plan on buying your way out.
Your money is worthless for this. This is the Day of God's Judgment—my wrath!
I care about sin with fiery passion—
A fire to burn up the corrupted world,
a wildfire finish to the corrupting people."

Zephaniah 1: 7-18

READY OR NOT...HERE I COME!

A children's game called Seek and Find or Hide and Seek by some is quite fun to play. It involves hiding and hearing the countdown knowing that the seeker is coming by the end of the final countdown. God has been seeking and finding us as the countdown started on the cross when Jesus declared it finished but many ignored the rules and missed the instructions that there is a limit to His time and The Great Judgement Day is approaching. The final countdown has started. The last round of seek and find is in play and those who ignore His call will be left bereft. Many have been tempted into hiding behind money and serving it as their god while others have taken on other pagan gods as their source. The technological advances have taken the countdown to the world so all can see instantly. The deep fakes from video to robotics have been created and ready for the Antichrist to use and abuse people with, as he fools their minds with false doctrine. Men and women have turned to technology to get their truths and even their scriptures so that many will easily be deceived. Doctrines will fail, money will fail, a day of Doom like no other is coming and only those who know in whom they believe will last. God's judgment on the rejection of His son's sacrifice will be profound. Softly, Jesus is calling…seeking us, knocking and calling…beckoning us to come home to His protection before the final wrath is poured out. Please do not wait. Please listen, hear, and act. It is time to come out of hiding and run to Jesus.

So get yourselves together. Shape up!
You're a nation without a clue
about what it wants.
Do it before you're blown away
like leaves in a windstorm,
Before God's Judgment-anger
sweeps down on you,
Before God's Judgment Day wrath
descends with full force.

* * *

Seek God, all you quietly disciplined people
who live by God's justice.
Seek God's right ways. Seek a quiet
and disciplined life.
Perhaps you'll be hidden on the
Day of God's anger.

Zephaniah 2: 1-3

QUIET DISCIPLINE!

Most people see me as an outgoing person who lives life large because I don't hide but the truth is that the real me is a quiet and deep person who has to discipline myself to be bold. I do not seek attention or need to be the center of attention as I prefer to operate quietly without notice while doing my thing. My devotionals that I do each day are personal and deep lessons that God is disciplining me through but part of my disciplining is to share His truth boldly so it appears to others that I live loud and large. I do like to be an encouraging person and a lifter of others. I do like to showcase the good in all and be the underskirt that holds the flower up to the sun. Yesterday I went around singing a kid's song called "I Am A Promise". It is because I am a possibility to leading others to my Savior. I love the quiet discourse with God and the steady hand of guidance but I also do not believe that we must hide who we are in Him. Recently a friend asked me how I had such an outgoing and open perspective and I told her the truth, that isn't me...the real me is quiet and a deep thinker. People perceive me to be a life of the party person because I stretch in Him and I enjoy who He is but my nature is actually not as vibrant as people believe. My sons are much like this too, as is my husband but while people perceive Wes and Gabe as quiet, deep people and John and I as open and outgoing, the truth is that all four of us are truly quiet and deep. A flower is a beautiful thing and not loud but as it quietly opens in the steadiness of timing, it exposes the beauty of God's creation within it. There are flowers that are bright and bold catching attention and others that are small in size and color but the purpose of them all is the same. All of them are created to procreate and glorify God through their beauty. These flowers attract the bees, birds and insects that allow our food to grow and the pollen in the petal is the substance that leads to new life. Do not let the perceptions of others determine who you are or will be. As I lay here on my back typing this message and hearing the music of hundreds of birds outside my patio door, I am reminded of my purpose. Our purpose just like the flower is to procreate God's love in the lives of others and glorify Him. Procreate means to bring forth life. Loving others openly through whatever you do is the way to go about life. If our love is perceived as loud or quiet, it doesn't matter. The truth is not about who you are as much as it is about who you glorify. I have received lots of honors in my life which are all blessings from a God who cares. I have also had lots of battles along the way, most of which are never publicly known. I seek God and His quiet discourse through my private disciplined life. My goal is to shape up so I can be a support system of His love and mercy to others and not leaves that are blown around in a windstorm. I choose to be His hand extended In whatever means He puts before me. Sometimes that is an uncomfortable stretching of things that are hard for me and you. Seek Him. Seek His right ways. All the other will happen as He desires it to be. Loving loudly may not feel natural to you but I have never heard a flower either, yet their fragrance and beauty overwhelms me. Do you soak in His presence? Let Him make you become who He desires you to be and all the rest will come.

"The accumulated sorrows of your exile will dissipate. I, your God, will get rid of them for you. You've carried those burdens long enough. At the same time, I'll get rid of all those who've made your life miserable. I'll heal the maimed; I'll bring home the homeless. In the very countries where they were hated they will be venerated. On Judgment Day I'll bring you back home—a great family gathering! You'll be famous and honored all over the world. You'll see it with your own eyes— all those painful partings turned into reunions!" God's Promise. Zephaniah 3:18-20

GOD'S PROMISE!

I, Your God....
Will dissipate your accumulated sorrows...
Will rid you of them completely...
Will release your burdens...
Will get rid of misery and all who caused it...
Will heal the maimed...
Will bring home the homeless...
Will venerate the hated...
Will bring you home...
Will prepare you a family gathering...
Will see that people honor you all over the world...
Will reunite you with those lost in painful partings...
God's Promise!

Wow! In two verses, most everyone on Earth can find their dreams, plans, goals or promises fulfilled. These are Godly promises to those who hide in Him, anchor in Him, and hold onto Him through the storms. The flower in this picture is smaller than my pinkie finger. It is almost impossible for my old eyes to see its potential or possibility because it is so small and these eyes are not that strong. But with the lenses of my camera pointed right at the flower and zoomed in, I can see the intricate beauty and perfection of dimensional structure. I could even see the seed, the future, the promise. Our eyes focus way too much on the oath directly in front of us so much that we fail to realize that no matter what the talking heads on the news say...we are full of promise. I am a promise, a possibility. I am a promise from God Himself full of potential and purpose. I may walk through life full of energy or discomfort but it does not lessen my promise. God's promise in us is not affected by us! God's promise is His promise and always will be. Our choice is whether we walk in promise or defeat. I remember the excitement in my boys' eyes after a good rain. They saw the promise of a mud puddle splash and all I saw was the puddle. Their joy however was contagious to the point that I too began to look forward to rainy days as a change and a potentially great moment of Time instead of dreading the mess and cleanup. I began to see the promise of adventure and excitement instead of dread and burden. Jesus says if we will give it to Him, He will take it and make it into something new. He will turn our sorrows into joy. Are we soaking in the rain and getting wet, miserable and whiny or are we dancing in the mud puddles of promise knowing He's got it all covered in His promises? I miss the mud puddles with my boys because they are grown and no longer eagerly awaiting the rainy puddles with joy. Bear with me though...I have decided that it is time I choose to dance in the rain of His promises and allow the mud puddles to speak to my soul of His promises. I will just have to take a shower in His love after I splash in the mud puddle of promises! How long has it been since we joyfully splashed in His promises without regard for our circumstances? I am tired of chasing rainbows and being spun around. It is time to lay it all at the feet of Jesus and go splash in His promises! Mud-pies here I come!

Light-seeds are planted in the souls of God's people, Joy-seeds are planted in good heart-soil.
Psalms 97:11

JOY STEALERS!

I was robbed today while I was sitting in my house and getting ready this morning. The crazy thing is that no one was here at the house with me but myself, and I am the one that let them in the door, not only did I let them in, but I invited them in. I knew they were coming by because they always do, but I rarely ever even look at them. Most of the time I go about my business, I have a quiet morning worshiping the Lord, I really rarely take the time to acknowledge those who sit outside my door.

They stand waiting and knocking, desiring to come in to steal and rob me blind and leave behind their sin. I realized today that I rarely ever even sit, on guard with my weapons at the ready to take care of them. I have the weapons. I'm trained to use the weapons. I know how to use the weapons. But today, I didn't even use them. I let those evil thoughts come in and steal things that were most precious to me. Things that I have held sacred for a long time, I let them steal. I opened the door and let them have things that keep my life with meaning. What is even worse, is that as they opened their boxes and bags to fill it up with my things, I helped them pack. My eyes are still itching and burning from the tears that I have cried, as I helped them pack my precious things into the bags to steal from me.

I would like to blame it on others, who told me to open that door and let in those evil deceivers who would steal from me over and over. I'd like to blame it on others who travel along with these guys, high-fiving them, cheering them and hanging with them through all of their worries and whys.

I would like to blame it on others but Blame is the name of one of them. He was the one who stole a precious gem. He came along with Worry and they both brought Fear in. The other guy who traveled along was Anger and he had a buddy too. He brought along a bag of bitterness he intended to leave behind. I was the one who allowed them in. I was the one who opened the door. I was the one who listened to them and helped pack my things over and over for them to steal.

I was robbed today. They came to steal my joy. I let them in and helped them pack through tears of grief overflowing. But then I heard a sweet, sweet song. The tune began to play. Greater is He that is in Me than those who came today. For even though I let them in and laid my weapons down. I had already been with Him in prayer and in the garden grounds. Jesus walked into that room and boy, did He take charge. He began to sing a melody so loud and sweet straight into my heart. Those evil guys began to quiver and then began to run. They took off down the road in haste because they knew He had come. I picked up all their baggage that they had left behind and put it in the burn pile so no others would be stunned. I unpacked my gems and cherished things-the most loved in the bags. I took them out and polished them with the songs that Jesus gave. He sat with me and helped me see the things they tried to take were never mine but belonged to Him just as I was His today. The Joy they smuggled and hid from me was found in Him, always. The love that had gotten buried in the bags was there reflected in His eyes as we polished it once again.

I'm telling you this story so you will not let them in. They knock and try each and every day but do not open that door. They come to steal something from you that doesn't even belong. You belong to Him. Pick up your weapons and shine the brass. Load that weapon with much love. For when they knock and try to steal, His word is weapon enough. If they've already come to you and stolen what you have, you can still go to where they are camped and take your joy back! Jesus is ready, just call His name. He will fight right by your side. And this Joy and Love, this peace and trust are too precious to allow them to have!

And then a little later, God-of-the-Angel-Armies
spoke out again:
"Take a good, hard look at your life.
Think it over.
You have spent a lot of money,
but you haven't much to show for it.
You keep filling your plates,
but you never get filled up.
You keep drinking and drinking and drinking,
but you're always thirsty.
You put on layer after layer of clothes,
but you can't get warm.
And the people who work for you,
what are they getting out of it?
Not much—
a leaky, rusted-out bucket, that's what."
That's why God-of-the-Angel-Armies said:
"Take a good, hard look at your life.
Think it over."

Haggai 1: 5-7

THINK IT OVER!

Made an impulsive decision to color my hair. Grabbed the box from the cabinet and now I have reddish-auburn hair. Was a little purple last night. Obviously I didn't look carefully at the box or think deeply before I jumped in and poured it on my hair as I would have noticed that the date was old on the box and if I had been more careful, I would've seen the color was called hot tamale. It is something I will definitely have to correct but also have to live with my decision for a bit. Sometimes we don't take a good hard look at things but rather jump into it and then wonder if it was the very best decision. I can truly say that I have been taking a hard look at my life lately. I have been examining my choices and investments of my time/efforts because as I age, they matter more. I can say that I have invested deeply in people. I love deeply, live fully and invest wholly in others. In Haggai, God speaks to the self indulgent people about their constant neediness and lack of contentment, comparing them to a leaky bucket. The constant need to have more is never satisfied because there isn't an evaluation of what is and isn't there. God is telling us to look at the complete mess of where we are placing our investments and think it over. What are we investing in? An infestation of self indulgent roaches because we have piled high junk we don't truly need or are we investing in the eternal? Where are we placing our values? What are we doing to tell others of Christ? Are we busy preparing for a future here and ignoring that times are drawing to an end? Are we investing and laying up wealth here for a rainy day instead of fulfilling lives with all we have now? How are you investing in those around you? Do they see you as sharing valuable insight with them or are you just a rusty, leaky, worn-out bucket dripping old moldy water? Are you filled with His living water that brings life and joy or are you wasting time/effort on futile things? Why all the questions today? Because God said...take a good, hard look at your life... Think it over! Are you spreading life or are you spreading death? What are your words and deeds doing to those who surround you? Think it over!

"'So get to work, Zerubbabel!'
–God is speaking.
"'Get to work, Joshua son of
Jehozadak–high priest!'
"'Get to work, all you people!'
–God is speaking.
"'Yes, get to work! For I am with you.'
The God-of-the-Angel-Armies is speak-
ing! 'Put into action the word I cove-
nanted with you when you left Egypt.
I'm living and breathing among you
right now. Don't be timid.
Don't hold back.'

Haggai 2: 4-5

GET TO WORK!

Ever have one of those days where it is hard to get moving? Today, my body feels lethargic and lazy, heavy, slumberous and then my devotional time starts with - God is Speaking, Get to Work. Alrighty then. He's not saying to go get dressed to go to work but rather Get to work in Him. He is insisting on us putting His living and breathing words into action rather than being timid and holding back. The halfway approach is what the people were giving in this story. They were charged with rebuilding God's temple and they were being mealy mouthed, grumbly and just not giving fully of themselves or their blessings. In fact, they had gotten so slumbering that they hadn't even noticed God's blessings. We are so guilty of this. We notice immediately when things don't go our way but the blessings we tend to ignore unless they are major miracles or changes. I mean, do we thank God for our beds to sleep in each night as we curl up in it or have we gotten so contented with what we have that we fail to see the blessings? Are we more concerned about our don't haves than the blessings we do have? Get up! Get moving! It is time to get out of our halfway, half hearted and slumbering routine of existence and begin to see His blessings and His provisions for what they truly are. It is time to recognize His grace and goodness and share the same with others around us. Don't hold back! Don't be timid! God is living and breathing in you! Rejoice! Celebrate! And put into action the things He has charged you to do. Get to work for He is with us!

In the eighth month of the second year in the reign of Darius, God's Message came to the prophet Zechariah son of Berechiah, son of Iddo: "God was very angry with your ancestors. So give to the people this Message from God-of-the-Angel-Armies: 'Come back to me and I'll come back to you. Don't be like your parents. The old-time prophets called out to them, "A Message from God-of-the-Angel-Armies: Leave your evil life. Quit your evil practices." But they ignored everything I said to them, stubbornly refused to listen.'

"And where are your ancestors now? Dead and buried. And the prophets who preached to them? Also dead and buried. But the Message that my servants the prophets spoke, that isn't dead and buried. That Message did its work on your ancestors, did it not? It woke them up and they came back, saying, 'He did what he said he would do, sure enough. We didn't get by with a thing.'"

Zechariah 1: 1-6

COME BACK!

Zechariah was a prophet of old who foretold much of what is coming in the future even now. At the time he delivered this message to God's people, he was referring to prophets before his time saying that the ancestors who experienced things and learned the lesson of God's ways are dead and buried along with the prophets who told them God's messages but God's word never dies. It keeps on going with life to revive. He says "Don't be like your parents" because he is trying to express that their parents learned things the hard way. Ignorance and stubborn refusal to listen or heed have been around since the beginning of time. God knew this about man and yet He created him anyway. God provided a way of escape from the culinary enticement of the delicious flavor of sin by giving us the will to fight the temptation and His word to guide/direct us, while His spirit dwells with us as a constant prophet warning us of our ways and choices. He wants us to have better sense than those who wandered in the desert for 40 years and had difficulty after difficulties because they refused to comply with His ways. He calls us to return to our first love-Him. "Come back to me and I will come back to you." I love a waterfall because it has such power, force, beauty and amazes us so. A waterfall Is nothing more than water droplets gathered together, forced through a fall as the land gives way under it directing it into a path of least resistance. What started as a placid flow of water in a struggling stream full of water droplets becomes a powerful force when it goes through a narrow fall of land forcing it to bind together powerfully. We are all water droplets of His love and mercy but when we bind together in tough falls or situations leaning not on things of Earth but trusting Him, the force of His love/mercy within us flows together as a powerful fall of water washing away and crashing the things around it that forced it into circumstances. The power of prayer between two or three of His droplets of love/mercy is never changing. We are a waterfall of epic proportions going through tough landscape building energy as we flow through Him and as we come back to Him in force, bound together, the droplets of prayer become a powerful force of change. Come back to Him and He will come back to us. Wow! These words have no end. He spoke them into the void just as He spoke Light which still exists as a force of nature. His words never come back void. Come back. Yield. Lean in. Come home. He's calling and telling us that He is still the same God. He does what He says He will do. We can do it the hard way as our ancestors or the easy way. We can flow through any situation bound to Him as a powerful waterfall....flow back to Him. Choose Him and He will Choose You!

Quiet, everyone! Shh! Silence before God. Something's afoot in his holy house. He's on the move!

Zechariah 2: 13

GOD'S MOVE!

As I drove so early in the morning, the city was eerily quiet with very little traffic. The hustle and bustle of traffic was not there and there was a hush that made it so calm as if the whole day was waiting to burst onto the scene. I imagine it as the quiet calm before God comes in. The start of a play when everyone hushes just prior to the scene opening is what I am reminded of today. Quiet, everyone! Shh! Silence-listen-He's about to make a move. Something is happening in His holy house. He's ready and about to step out to tell His son to call for His bride. Don't doubt, get quiet and listen. Don't fear, get quiet and listen. Don't watch the world and turn her way, watch and listen to God. Don't let the hustle and bustle of all things stir your spirit into a fuss, get quiet and listen. Be still. He is God! Something is afoot. It isn't about you. It is about Him. He is on the move. Make the way. Shh! Quiet your spirit. God is on the move. Silence before Him so you can tune to what He is doing!

God's Angel then charged Joshua, "Orders from God-of-the-Angel-Armies: 'If you live the way I tell you and remain obedient in my service, then you'll make the decisions around here and oversee my affairs. And all my attendants standing here will be at your service."

'Careful, High Priest Joshua—both you and your friends sitting here with you, for your friends are in on this, too! Here's what I'm doing next: I'm introducing my servant Branch. And note this: This stone that I'm placing before Joshua, a single stone with seven eyes'—Decree of God-of-the-Angel-Armies—'I'll engrave with these words: "I'll strip this land of its filthy sin, all at once, in a single day."

"'At that time, everyone will get along with one another, with friendly visits across the fence, friendly visits on one another's porches.'"

Zechariah 3: 6-10

IF!

The situation was tough and the schedule impossible. Everything was upside down and twisted up inside as I wondered how it was going to work. Then I remembered the charge: If my people who are called by my name will humble themselves and pray, then I will heal, move, work....the promises are true and the time-lines infinite but we must remove the If. Our conversation turned to things of the impossible as he stated to me, it isn't that I don't trust God or know that He can but I am not sure He will. Brother, sister and friend, that is a lack of trust! What has happened is that we have walked into the place of mortal thought and out of the mind of God. Disappointed times in our lives when we feel God failed to perform as we wanted is what leads to this mindset. That friend, sister, husband, father or other loved one that suffered and wasn't healed here on Earth despite the prayers and belief; that impossible situation that exploded in our face because God didn't perform the miracle we felt was required; that hope/dream that got dusty and failed to mature seemed to indicate that God just is an Iffy God. I have heard people say it over and over. I do not doubt that He can because I have seen that but I am not sure He Will because I have been disappointed in the past...that is the Joshua difference. Joshua and Caleb were two of the 12 who went into the land and saw the impossible. Understand that these 12 men had seen God do so many impossibilities in miraculous means from parting the Red Sea to providing water from a rock in the middle of the desert. They had lived with His daily provision of food from Heaven. They had been given the law of the Covenant from God but only two looked at the land and saw the promise while the other ten only saw the IF! IF stands for I Fail to believe! It is a lack of trust in who He is. In Zechariah, he sees the fourth vision of Joshua receiving new clothes and a turban then God charges Joshua with the IF. The IF is the power we walk in today. Jesus is the Branch, the Stone with seven eyes, spirits, going about as the all seeing and the Lamb who made the impossible into the possible but the IF is our charge. If you live the way I tell you and remain obedient in my service, then you will make the decisions and oversee God's affairs. Joshua was able to command the sun to be still and stop time because he knew the IF. He abided in the IF. The I Fail, but for God. Joshua knew the same thing the man who desired healing for His daughter knew and recognized in his words, I believe, but God help my unbelief. We are just like all mortals who have a God sized hole in our souls. When we fail to fill it, the unbelieving IF creeps in to sit in the corner growing and feeding our minds on every impossible thing. "It's not doubt, but I don't think God is over everything," he said. "Some things He expects us to do." Nope! That's the IF talking. The I Fail to believe, the I Fail to live and walk in obedience, the I Fail to see, the I Fail to live the Way, the Truth and the Life. The lady with the issue of blood walked in failure of all to stop her bleeding and she walked in a different IF. Her walk was if I can touch Him, then I know He will. I failed to get help from any other source but I know He will...not He can but He will. Today, we tend to meander from place to place in our lives. We walk in the land of giants with our slingshot declaring war and winning, then go home in victory only to listen to the talking heads of man's divination and allow the If to creep into the mind. We tend to our ways and allow the voices around us to speak out in negativity. Note that when God charged Joshua, He gave Him a responsibility for those who surround him. He said Careful for both you and your friends sitting here with you, are in on this. You choose those friends. If you live the way God tells you and remain obedient in His service then you too can command the sun to stop and it will because you will oversee God's affairs but what IF are you walking in: The if I can touch Him or the if He will mentality? What made the Joshua difference? The "as for me and my house, we Will serve the Lord". It is a choice. If.
Two little letters that make all the difference.

He said, "What do you see?" I answered, "I see a lampstand of solid gold with a bowl on top. Seven lamps, each with seven spouts, are set on the bowl. And there are two olive trees, one on either side of the bowl."

Going back to the vision, the Messenger-Angel said, "The seven lamps are the eyes of God probing the dark corners of the world like searchlights." "And the two olive trees on either side of the lampstand?" I asked. "What's the meaning of them? And while you're at it, the two branches of the olive trees that feed oil to the lamps—what do they mean?" He said, "You haven't figured that out?" I said, "No, sir." He said, "These are the two who stand beside the Master of the whole earth and supply golden lamp oil worldwide."
Zechariah 4:2-3, 8-14

WHAT DO YOU SEE?

A vision, a thought, a dream, a feeling, a prayer, an answer...all a part of communication with God. But what is a vision truly? I struggled to see all my life so vision to me is a priority. In scripture vision is often compared to light or a lamp. In this vision, picture an old-timey lamp stand with candle style lamps set on a golden bowl that has a channel of oil to feed the lamps. The two olive trees on either side drip oil into that bowl continuously. These are all symbolic images of the light of God in Heaven pouring out and supplying light to all. The seven lamps are the eyes of God probing the dark corners of the Earth like searchlights looking for that lost one to come home. Lots of people have opinions and interpretations of the prophecy and vision recorded here but the thought that God placed in my heart is His vision. His word says that without vision, the people will perish. There is great danger in not seeing God. There is great harm that befalls us when we fail to recognize His hand due to the fogginess of the world. There is great devastation and death in our spirits when we fail to recognize the small things that God is doing in our lives as massive underground work laying foundations of greatness. For when we disregard the work He is doing, we disregard Him. When we fail to look through His eyes to see the one, the importance of that one moment or purpose, we fall short of His design. One puzzle piece missing leaves the puzzle incomplete. One matters. One moment. One word. One thought. One deed. One action. One step or misstep. We have become a people who expect huge things in microseconds rather than realizing that the golden oil of God comes from the one olive that stays on the branch drawing from The Vine supplying oil one drop at a time to the bowl which feeds the lamps that light the world. What do you see? Are you so foggy in your vision that you fail to see God in the small things? A picture recently posted which has been around for a while of a visual perception exercise shows at once glance a young woman looking away and at another an elderly woman looking down. Both are a vision of the woman and both are real but perception is different and some people have to look very hard to see the truth in the picture. The photo behind this scripture is a shot of the evening light casting a golden hue on the mountains, burnishing them into nuggets of gold. What is the value of that one moment? That one photo? That one second of time? What is the value of one? The value of one is whole. A fraction of a second can change a life. Have you figured it out now? What do you see? Quit devaluing the one. Begin to embrace the one moment, the one prayer, the one as that fraction of a second that God can turn into a miracle. Quit allowing that one thing to derail your day, minute, week, year or life. Take that one and make it count. You are one. You matter. Each fraction of each second of your life in all that you do counts because it is incomplete without that one. Be the one who stands beside the Master of the whole Earth supplying golden lamp oil worldwide through your one moment that you get to be His light. Be the diamond that takes that light and reflects it around the Earth. Your moment counts.

What do you see?

I looked up again and saw–surprise!–
a book on the wing!
A book flying!
The Messenger-Angel said to me,
"What do you see now?"
I said, "I see a book flying, a huge book–
thirty feet long and fifteen wide!"
He told me,
"This book is the verdict going out worldwide against
thieves and liars. The first half of the book disposes
of everyone who steals; the second half takes care of
everyone who lies. I launched it"
–Decree of God-of-the-Angel-Armies–
"and so it will fly into the house of
every thief and every liar.
It will land in each house and tear it down,
timbers and stones."

Zechariah 5: 1-4

THE BOOK OF TIME FLIES!

       Yesterday as I went through old photos, the truth of the old adage 'Time flies' became fully evident. Time is a huge book that flies going out and proclaims the truth despite all we would like to hide. Time is the one thing that passes and which we can never get back again. Sacred moments they all are. Each moment a witness against the next for the future. My dad used to tell me that each moment I looked into the mirror I should see the mother of the woman I would become and honestly I never understood what he was saying until a few years ago as I started becoming that woman I had mothered all those years. The things we tell ourselves and the choices we make last eternity. We can choose to feed upon the principles of God's word as recorded in His book or we can write into the annals of our own way with lies that steal our time and create a false reality but the truth will remain. Time is a thief as BB King writes it:

"I woke up this morning and looked at my life
Filled with so much sorrow and grief
And in my troubled mind
I could see through all my strife
That time is only a thief
Yes time is a thief
That will steal your tomorrows
And leave you only yesterday
Yes time is a thief
That will rob you of your years
Your youth the only ransom you can pay
So treasure each little moment
Don't let a single minute slip away
Because time is a thief
That will rob you of your years
And never return one yesterday
Oh time is a thief
That will rob you of your years
And never return one yesterday"

We are not promised tomorrow on this Earth. We are promised eternity. What and who you live for matters. Creating lies to steal time only gets the "book" thrown at you by God Himself. You cannot steal time no matter how full of lies you stuff it. Believe me, many people have tried. The fountain of youth doesn't exist on this Earth and no matter how many tummy tucks and facelifts one has, time still marches on and the life of lies and the power struggle still exists as the thieves of this world steal and destroy in the name of progress. I look at many of our government leaders and truly I see them with pity. The book of time is hitting their lives with its huge length and width. They have lied and stolen all they can to heap success and power upon themselves only to have the book of time reveal the truth that they too are nothing but thieves and liars desperate to cheat time but no matter what they did and who they hurt, the book of time flies straight and true. Their names will not be remembered or revered for the book from God flies true destroying their corrupt lies and tearing down their stolen stories. It isn't only them though. The book as seen in this vision strikes at every thief and liar as time knows no difference. Only what we do for God will last. Nothing we build or lay up as treasure will still stand the test of time except what we place into the hands of Truth. Jesus is The Way, The Truth, The Life and no man comes to The Father except through Him. We can pretty it up for Facebook and our friends but the falseness will not stand the test of time. The photos stare back at me through the eyes of time telling me the truth of eternity. We only have one life to live. This life has purpose, to share the Love of God through His Son Jesus who sacrificed His Time to make The Way where there was no way. The lies and booty that has been stolen will not make it past the curtain of time. The Truth is The Way, The Life. I picture this book of time as it flies on the wings of truth into each life destroying the lies and tearing down that which was built on theft. Zechariah foretold this in his 6th vision. The book of time is flying straight and true into each of our lives. For some it will see The blood of Jesus and know that our sins are covered and our names are recorded in the book itself. For others, the book will reveal all destructive theft and vicious lies in the name of power as it wipes out the lineage and legacy of those who stole/lied to achieve power. My name will not ever be recorded in a history book but it will be in the Lamb's Book of Life. As this book of time flies from home to home and household to household, The Truth speaks from its pages declaring despite it all, He forgives. Time is not merciful but Jesus is.

Choose wisely.

God-of-the-Angel-Armies gave me this Message for them, for all the people and for the priests: "When you held days of fasting every fifth and seventh month all these seventy years, were you doing it for me? And when you held feasts, was that for me? Hardly. You're interested in religion, I'm interested in people.

"There's nothing new to say on the subject. Don't you still have the message of the earlier prophets from the time when Jerusalem was still a thriving, bustling city and the outlying countryside, the Negev and Shephelah, was populated?

[This is the message that God gave Zechariah.]

Well, the message hasn't changed. God-of-the-Angel-Armies said then and says now:

"'Treat one another justly.
Love your neighbors.
Be compassionate with each other.
Don't take advantage of widows, orphans, visitors, and the poor.
Don't plot and scheme against one another—that's evil.'

Zechariah 7: 4-10

THE PEOPLE MESSAGE!

The sign leans after the tornado but most don't notice it. The pole it is fixed on is level and the sign reads the same. There are some broken panels but overall the damage isn't noticeable.

We as people get stuck. The sameness is comforting and easy. But we tend to ignore problems when they "look" the same. We tend to fail to pay attention because we have always done it that way and we get stuck in ruts of sameness without realizing that the message of God hasn't changed but it is supposed to grow. I am fascinated by the mint I have in my garden tub. It has grown profusely with only a little water and sun, none of which required my attention. It is so rooted that it reproduces consistently no matter what happens to it. It has grown and grown despite weathering storms and hail, drought and cold. It goes deep in winter and rests then when the sun shines on it, it produces beautifully. I keep it in a garden pot because I know it is an extremely reproductive plant that spreads like crazy, much like the wisteria in the picture. They are rooted and from there they grow underground to the next place of growth. Their system of reproduction isn't visible to our eyes except in the above ground growth. God's message hasn't changed and should be deeply rooted in each of us. In Zechariah 7, He reminds us that His message has not changed. Treating each other justly. Loving our neighbors. Being compassionate with each other and not taking advantage of others as well as not plotting and scheming are all the results of His Love as growth in our lives. His message never changes. It is level, fixed and rooted. There is nothing new to it but it should be growing and rooting deeper in us. It should be reproducing under ground so that new branches and outreaches of His love are evident in us always. We need to get past doing things the same way in a way of religion and realizing that His love isn't limited by location nor time. His love knows no boundaries. His love is this Message. When we hold revivals or days of fasting or other religious activities, we need to examine the why. Is it out of habit or love? Is it out of habit, expectations or love that we attend church? Is it out of love that we do the things we do or are we just tinkling brass? The wind blows and nothing changes. I hear the wind chime and know it is blowing but I cannot see the difference. The wind of God is blowing through us and God is wanting to use us to make a difference in the lives of those we touch but we must be willing to be more than just a wind chime that sings of His presence but stays fixed in the place it is hung. We must be a noticeable difference in the lives of others or we are nothing more than a festival or ritual celebration. What are we doing to Love our neighbors? How are we demonstrating His compassion to others? Are we doing more for the widows, orphans and the poor? Do visitors feel God's presence and love? Are we treating each other justly and purely? Are we playing the game of life or planning a celebration of eternity? The message is the same. It is rooted within us. Are we growing or are we just standing, waiting on the winds to blow us?

A Message from God-of-the-Angel-Armies:

"Do the problems of returning and rebuilding by just a few survivors seem too much? But is anything too much for me? Not if I have my say."

Zechariah 8: 6

GOD'S SAY....!

Do your problems seem too much? The tree was burdened by the heavy load of leaves and acorns so that it bowed down low from the weight. When the storm came, it made the ground very wet and the weight of the leaves doubled. Then the wind pulsed, pushing and the tree tried to stand firm but its roots were too shallow and the ground too moist and the weight too much. The tree fell over, crushing the building. Waking up to the crash, my friend hoped it was a tree in the woods but alas the tree had fallen through her garage apartment claiming all. The idea of rebuilding with little to no means on a retirement income was overwhelming. She had very little help and the deck seemed stacked against her until she remembered whose child she was. Rather than sinking into the pit of depression that yawned in front of her, she began to call upon God. He heard her. She continued in prayer as she moved around the room to get back to her bedroom where she had an epiphany. He had kept her safe. Yes, her apartment was probably a complete loss but she was fine. As she walked back into her room and saw the immense size and breadth of that tree, she heard a noise. She looked down and at her feet was a nest of baby squirrels. They were snuggled together in the branch of the tree that had landed on a padded surface. She began to cry as she realized that nothing is too big for our God. Situations look impossible from cancer diagnosis to ruined homes but God is the God of Angel Armies. Nothing is too much for God. Let Him have His say. His say, is that He is more than enough. His say is that He is the I AM! His say is that He is our counselor, our prince of peace, our mighty God. He says He is the Lion of Judah, the Stone upon which all foundations are laid. He says that He is our Father, Husband and Provider. He says that He can do ALL things. Scripture lists almost 1000 names for God!

So the question is, is there anything too much for Him or is it because we quit asking? My friend looked at those baby squirrels and saw a God who cares. She could've looked at them and saw another task and like the tree, crashed as the weight and wind became too much but she saw the God who laid those babies on a pillow though their world had upended. She saw the God who cares. The road to rebuilding is still long and her life is still disrupted but she chose hope and walking in His love. She chose to let God have His say. It seemed a long road that was rocky and hard but she decided to reach up and trust. Sometimes we feel stretched too thin, overwhelmed and feeling like giving in. But if we will let God have His say, nothing is too much for Him. Allow God to have His Say! Nothing is too much for Him! Give it all to Him! He's got you!

Then God will come into view,
his arrows flashing like lightning!
Master God will blast his trumpet
and set out in a whirlwind.
God-of-the-Angel-Armies will protect
them—all-out war,
The war to end all wars,
no holds barred.
Their God will save the day. He'll rescue
them. They'll become like sheep, gentle
and soft, Or like gemstones in a crown,
catching all the colors of the sun.
Then how they'll shine! shimmer! glow!
the young men robust, the young
women lovely!

Zechariah 9: 14-17

SHINE! SHIMMER! GLOW!

"Why is it so much work to serve God?" she asked. The question totally surprised me because it had never crossed my mind that serving God was work. "I feel like Cinderella waiting for the Prince to rescue her. I thought serving God would be fun but it is always work." My heart broke. She was going through the motions of religion but she hadn't become intimate with her Savior. Many of us grew up in religious views of what you can or cannot do to be a Christian instead of understanding who He is. Others think He is an indulgent parent who will tolerate anything because of His love. The truth is that He is both and neither of these. He is God. Yes, if you are like those who cleave to religion as the dos and don'ts then you will see it as a pattern of working to achieve a goal and if you think God tolerates anything then you'll likely miss out because you are not respecting or fearing who He is. God is the God of judgment and fierceness enforcing His law but He is also the rescuing Prince and the Loving Father! God is God. Relationship to Him is personal, intimate and evolving. But He is the same yesterday, today and forever. He is not a God who changes in respect to His laws just because culturally it is popular. Sin is still sin and He abhors it. An undisciplined child is unruly and difficult to deal with for the parent. Children need direction, instruction, discipline and love, lots of love. For the direction and instructions come from Love and a desire to protect and save but also the discipline allows the child to grow into the person who is able to manage their own impulses and make good decisions from their learned wise instruction. When we first begin to walk with the Lord, we do not really trust Him as deeply as we should. He longs for us to understand so we can, but it takes instruction and teaching through the hard times of rescue and serving-the hard places to develop us, but He is there loving us and guiding us as we press in. You may feel like a Cinderella or Cinderfella as you walk through the fires of life but the difference is that the Prince of Peace is right there with you. He is seeking you and finding you as you seek and find Him. He is closer than a brother and better than a BFF. He is more than an indulgent Father because He cares for you but He will not tolerate the lies being told about Him nor the falsehoods of religious fallacies. Just as Jesus came and was despised on Earth by the world religions so He is despised truly, though not always openly, by many of them now. They use His love as a cover for their lies. His love covers a multitude of sins when they are repented of but not during the sin and He certainly will not tolerate it in His house. If you feel like Cinderella waiting on the prince, I suggest you take some time and spend it with Him. Get into His word, talk with Him in prayer, praise Him in song and then you will see that He is as close as the mention of His name. The jewels of His crown shimmer, shine and glow no brighter than those He has redeemed. He has rescued us already. We are not in this world alone waiting for rescue because He has already come and gave His life to redeem us. The Prince came down and offered His life for His bride. His life was given and thus, redeemed Her. She now holds the place of authority in His absence and all things in Earth are under her dominion in His name. But God will not tolerate the disdain and disrespect that has been attributed to His name nor the hatred and lies about His bride. Jesus will come into view boldly with the sound of the trumpet and all of His bride will be caught away. Then the war to end all wars will ensue with God riding to the rescue and saving the day...He will polish them as gemstones so they sparkle, shimmer and shine in the glow of His glory. Dust off those heavy bands and lift up your Holy hands...you are God's children and it is time to praise the Lord.

Pray to God for rain—it's time for the spring rain—
to God, the rainmaker,
Spring thunderstorm maker,
maker of grain and barley.
"Store-bought gods babble gibberish.
Religious experts spout rubbish.
They pontificate hot air.
Their prescriptions are nothing but smoke.
And so the people wander like lost sheep,
poor lost sheep without a shepherd.
I'm furious with the so-called shepherds.
They're worse than billy goats, and I'll treat them like goats."
God-of-the-Angel-Armies will step in
and take care of his flock, the people of Judah.
He'll revive their spirits,
make them proud to be on God's side.
God will use them in his work of rebuilding,
use them as foundations and pillars,
Use them as tools and instruments,
use them to oversee his work.
They'll be a workforce to be proud of, working as one,
their heads held high, striding through swamps and mud,
Courageous and vigorous because God is with them,
undeterred by the world's thugs.

Zechariah 10: 1-5

UNDETERRED!

   Keeping our heads to the grindstone of daily work whether it be physical or mental can be exhausting to say the least. In Zechariah 10, God is expressing His frustration with the "shepherds" who have caused confusion and conflict in the "sheep" by using other means rather than His word to draw and direct. He calls them worse than billy goats and says He will treat them as such. Shepherds are the pastoral care staff that have been called to lead and direct the sheep on the path but when they act as billy goats, they are playing around and wandering off course where the sheep get confused about what is/isn't God's truth. God calls it using store bought gibberish, rubbish and prescriptions of smoke. But then He says that He Himself will step in to take care of His flock. He will revive our spirits and make us proud to be on God's side. He says He will use us as tools and instruments and firm us into a workforce to be proud of with our heads held high and full of confidence as we stride through swamps and mud to rebuild His kingdom. Because of Him being with us, we will not be deterred by the thugs of this world. If you are feeling discouraged today, if the weight seems too much to bear, call upon Jesus for a fresh anointing and His rain to fall as a spring rain upon you. He will be there. He will come and refresh you to make you courageous and vigorous in the Love of Christ so that the thugs and problems of this world will not deter you from His path.

War Bulletin:
God's Message concerning Israel, God's Decree—the very God who threw the skies into space, set earth on a firm foundation, and breathed his own life into men and women: "Watch for this: I'm about to turn Jerusalem into a cup of strong drink that will have the people who have set siege to Judah and Jerusalem staggering in a drunken stupor.

Zechariah 12: 1-2

WAR BULLETIN!

The warnings are posted and they are dire. Severe weather is expected and since we just went through a tornado weeks ago, the message speaks loud and clear. I have always been a nervous weather person but for sure I feel it much more intensely since I had all this metal installed in my body. As the pressure builds, my bones in my spine send signals to my brain warning it. In Zechariah, God has foretold the time coming and the warnings are clearly laid out. In chapter 11, the doom of the nations and the people when God removes His hand is profound and the last couple of verses describe our current leadership of government clearly. But chapter 11 portends what happens before the war and the War Bulletin is how chapter 12 begins. God's decree. The most powerful and mighty who threw the skies into space that we are still exploring and being amazed at daily. This God who set earth or the land upon a firm foundation in a fixed position of exact measure to get the right amount of light/dark and the round principles of gravity and balance gives a decree. The God who breathed His very life into us warns us to prepare: Watch this! This is the signal of war.; the war decree of wars that will end all wars.

A friend of mine recently posted from Kyiv that since they have been in war with bombs and warnings daily for over a year now, people now ignore the signals and signs. The warnings have grown old and the bombing has taken so much that the people are war weary. The warnings are posted. We know the value of a warning, for the last tornado was unwarned as it occurred between a radar cycle. We pay attention now to weather bulletins. I wonder if the same can be said of this warning from God? He has called, loved, beckoned and died for us. He has suffered indignity after blasphemous lies. He has tolerated the foolishness and lack of gratitude for so long. The Holy Shepherd has had enough with the foolishness and when He unleashes His wrath...it is like pouring a strong dose of retribution out upon the world. Warning: War Bulletin: are we listening and paying attention?

"Sword, get moving against my shepherd,
against my close associate!"
Decree of God-of-the-Angel-Armies.
"Kill the shepherd! Scatter the sheep!
The back of my hand against even the lambs!
All across the country"–God's Decree–
"two-thirds will be devastated
and one-third survive.
I'll deliver the surviving third to the
refinery fires.
I'll refine them as silver is refined,
test them for purity as gold is tested.
Then they'll pray to me by name
and I'll answer them personally.
I'll say, 'That's my people.'
They'll say, 'God–my God!'"

Zechariah 13: 7-9

REFINING FIRE!

No one wants to think of God as a fierce God until they need Him to defend them. No one wants to think of God as being God of judgment until they need a judge. People rail against the law and rules and the people that uphold these until they need the law, rules, police and lawyers to uphold them. Refining fire is God's way of bringing us into His Holiness. People have used the word sanctification but many do not understand that word. Sanctification is a refining fire that brings us closer to the one who is purifying us for His glory. It is the process by which the draught is all burned up and we are fully committed to Him. We often go through trials and hardships that are a part of this refining but we fight against it and avoid it, begging God to take it away. The process of refining isn't fun for that which is being refined because it requires change and change is hard and uncomfortable. It is often unpredictable and painful as well. Think, 2/3rds will be just gone while 1/3rd will survive but will have to go through the incredibly hard process of refining. God says He will refine them as silver and test for purity as with gold. That process involves lots of time and testing. That process requires melting and reshaping, remolding and remaking. The process of refining isn't for the faint of heart. It is a tough process of allowing the lead jeweler to be the master and the metal to be pliable. See, refining causes pliability. It melts and reshapes causing the metal to become a completely different look and feel than it was prior. It is a process of self-deprecation and lifting up only of Him. After the refining and only after, God says they can call me by name and I will answer. What is the refining process you are experiencing? Are you becoming more pliable in the Master Jeweler's hand or are you fighting the process? Refining isn't easy but when it is accomplished, the jeweler then marks the creation with his name and God does the same. The jewelry is set apart as very special and significant because it bears the name of the Creator and he recognizes His creation. God calls us by the name He gave us. He renamed those who withstood the refining fire. Abram became Abraham. Jacob became Israel. Sarai became Sarah and Hadassah became Esther. He knows your name. He calls your name through the refining to look only to Him through the fire! What kind of masterpiece will you become? Yielded to Him? Called by His name and His purpose? Refined and highly valued or full of the world and burned up because the value was depleted by the lack of yield?

What a Day that will be! No more cold nights—in fact, no more nights! The Day is coming—the timing is God's—when it will be continuous day. Every evening will be a fresh morning.
What a Day that will be! Fresh flowing rivers out of Jerusalem, half to the eastern sea, half to the western sea, flowing year-round, summer and winter! God will be king over all the earth, one God and only one.
What a Day that will be!

Zechariah 14: 6-9

CONTINUOUS DAY!

Day and night as opposites and in scriptures often signal a symbolic meaning. Day stands for that which is good, holy and joyful while night stands for evil, darkness and sorrow. In this chapter of Zechariah, God is revealing the Days of no more nights. The Day the Son reigns supreme as the sun of all the Earth. Night never comes because Joy is sitting in His presence. It is hard for us to imagine a world of no sorrow, pain, sickness or death because we have grown used to it. We have lived so long in the sorrows and evil with sin beating at us that we have forgotten that this isn't the way God designed things to be! He designed this world in beautiful harmony. He designed a paradise for mankind. We are His design. He is desirous of a deep and lasting relationship with us. I was just discussing vacation and a trip with some others and someone said I am so excited that I am already packing while I thought, that is still months away...but the excitement was contagious. Just imagine if we-knowing Jesus is coming any day to take us to Heaven-a place of eternal day... could get so excited about it that we spread our contagious joy of soon and very soon. An all expense paid eternal vacation to paradise where there will be no more sorrow, pain or darkness... only continuous day-wow! What a thought!

"I am honored all over the world. And there are people who know how to worship me all over the world, who honor me by bringing their best to me. They're saying it everywhere: 'God is greater, this God-of-the-Angel-Armies.' "A curse on the person who makes a big show of doing something great for me—an expensive sacrifice, say—and then at the last minute brings in something puny and worthless! I'm a great king, God-of-the-Angel-Armies, honored far and wide, and I'll not put up with it!"
Malachi 1:11, 14

ANGEL ARMIES!

The last few days, all eyes have been in the skies as the airplane performances have been quite spectacular. The AirShow of sheer talent at directing an aircraft safely through tricks is quite amazing and awe inspiring but they have nothing on our God. As God speaks in Malachi to the people, He asks a question of us today too: where is My Honor? In the midst of the coming and going, we often forget or misplace the one thing that God says is first and foremost: Honor, having no other god before Him. As I gazed into the Heavens, it appeared as if there were angels flying through the clouds. I know others will say this is the after of the jet streams left by the performance on this clear day but I couldn't stop myself from asking, where is His honor? Many people dressed up, got special outfits, prepared well in advance, waited hours to get into the airfield to see these phenomenal skills of flying but many sacrificed their time with God to do so. I wonder how many of us do the same with all the preparation and special clothes and waiting in anticipation for going into the House of God where we approach the Holy of Holies? I wonder how many of us prepare ourselves in advance by sacrificing the waiting time of hours in His word and worship as we anticipate what He will do when He comes to show us His glory, when He passes through our gathering, when He touches us through His Spirit? Do not take this in a poor manner of me attacking those who attended an airshow or worked at a job and missed church. If you do, you miss the point Or perhaps deflect it purposely. As God spoke to the people through Malachi, they were putting on a show of going to church and offering their best but in reality, the best was not what they offered. They let others see them and then they did the opposite. They appeared to be doing and giving all but in reality they had lost respect for God and were giving only a show. The thing about an airshow is for the pilots, their best is required or it results in death as we saw in Dallas not too long ago. They cannot play as if it is their best and give less or else they risk their lives. We too must realize that God requires our best. We cannot play at giving our best then switch to half or less because God will not tolerate that disrespect. Am I giving God the best of me or is He getting leftovers when I am tired and worn out? Am I prioritizing God and giving Him quality time, effort and gifts? The first tenth of my abilities, finances, talents and thoughts or am I displeasing Him by giving Him the dregs from my coffee cup of life at the end of a day? He sees the difference and He knows our hearts. This God of the Angel Armies calls to you..."where are you? Why are you hiding? Your sin against me is why I sent my Son to die for you. I forgive you. Come into my rest. Bring your offerings-your very best. Stay with me. Spend time with me and see all the things I do and will do."

And here's a second offense: You fill the place of worship with your whining and sniveling because you don't get what you want from God. Do you know why? Simple. Because God was there as a witness when you spoke your marriage vows to your young bride, and now you've broken those vows, broken the faith-bond with your vowed companion, your covenant wife. God, not you, made marriage. His Spirit inhabits even the smallest details of marriage. And what does he want from marriage? Children of God, that's what. So guard the spirit of marriage within you. Don't cheat on your spouse.
Malachi 2:13-15

THE FAITH-BOND!

I love this photo of two sun drenched clouds that swirled together appearing as two hands held fast. Handfasting, tying the knot and a wedding ceremony are all ways of saying that someone has chosen to make a faith-bond with another or vow before God to hold fast the covenant they make before God in marriage. For us, marriage has been over 26 years. I don't say that to brag. I say that because each day is a choice of two very different people, to stand in faith with the other and God, committing to be true to the other, trustworthy and faithful. The hardest part of a faith-bond is not believing that the other person will do their part. The hardest part is the daily choice. Some hours and days, the choice is easy but others are filled with temptation and trial. Today's constant desire for technology challenges this too. There is a constant demand upon time, attention, faithfulness and loyalty in our hands. Lewd images are everywhere. Lewd words, descriptions, and visual stimuli tempt everyone daily. It is a choice to remain faithful to the vow you made to God and spouse or will make. God's Spirit inhabits even the smallest details of marriage and while it is easy to see/decry someone who is unfaithful in their sexual behavior, it is harder but just as hurtful if they break their faithfulness in other ways. I've watched many a marriage torn apart by lies and deception but more are torn apart by neglect. Neglect is when you do not take deliberate time to spend with the person you vowed to spend your best of you with. When you make a vow before God to become one, you make a vow to prioritize that person over everything and everyone else including career, past time, family, and personal dreams. You make a vow before God which ushered a spirit of marriage into your lives to keep you bound. That inner voice that says "put up that video game, tablet, FB or other distractions and spend time with your spouse" is the spirit of marriage warning you of impending issues if you ignore it. God calls the abandonment of marriage as an offense. Why? Because God takes offense at anything that hurts the innocent and what God desires of marriage is children of God. Children raised in a secure loving home that knows God, know God early and walk with Him. When was the last time you took measure of your faith bond? Are you heeding the still small voice warning you that there are areas you must address? Are you busy whining that things aren't going the way you want but have ignored the person you vowed to prioritize? It's simple. Shore up your faith bond with the love of your life. Spend time, full attention and cherish them. I see those who have loved and lost their spouse. Their advice to us is to live more fiercely and deeply. Don't waste time on petty disagreements but cherish each moment. Catch the sunrise together and the sunset. Prioritize your faith-bond, your marriage or your relationship before God. Measure it by His standards. Would God be pleased with how we are honoring the faith bond we pledged before Him?
 me. Spend time with me and see all the things I do and will do."

"Yes, I'm on my way to visit you with Judgment. I'll present compelling evidence against sorcerers, adulterers, liars, those who exploit workers, those who take advantage of widows and orphans, those who are inhospitable to the homeless–anyone and everyone who doesn't honor me." A Message from God-of-the-Angel-Armies.

God-of-the-Angel-Armies said, "They're mine, all mine. They'll get special treatment when I go into action. I treat them with the same consideration and kindness that parents give the child who honors them. Once more you'll see the difference it makes between being a person who does the right thing and one who doesn't, between serving God and not serving him."

Malachi 3: 5, 17-18

TO HONOR IS TO SERVE!

It is no surprise to me that honoring God is stated in Malachi as the difference in special treatment of considerable action and kindness by God to those who serve Him. What may be a surprise to some is those that dishonor Him are listed in the same list as deadly sins like taking advantage of others, exploitation, sorcerers, adulterers and liars. To serve with honor means to serve without questioning why. To serve with honor means to trust that the person who has been put in charge of you or is in charge of you knows what is best. To serve with honor means that there is a level of respect, for that person, to where you do not question his authority, ability, nor his willingness to do what is right in your situation. When the Cadet first enters the military, one of the first things that is trained into them is to respect the authority of the person who is in charge. The reason why this is important is because many times they will question why they are doing something because they don't see the full picture. When someone questions the authority who has given orders that are in line with their word, there is conflict and confusion because the person questioning the authority doesn't know why the order was given. I am not condoning doing things blindly, especially in a culture that does not honor God, and with all of the hidden agendas that we see. However, God is affirming over and over that those who honor his authority with respect and serve him in that honor are the ones who will be blessed. We do not serve a God who is a Man that is flawed and has weaknesses, that is seeking power and authority and privilege and monetary gain. We serve a God, who already has all those things, and was willing to sacrifice all of those things, and his very own life to come and save us from our mistakes. If we serve a God who was willing to give up everything to serve us, then why are we not willing to honor him in our service? Why do we question his authority? This is the same God, who created everything that we see and this is the same God that created the sun, the moon, the stars, and the planets. This is the same God, who said let there be light, and there was light. This is the same God who ordered oceans to roll back so people could walk through. This is the same God, who ordered the mouths of lions to be closed and the three Hebrew children to walk freely in a fiery furnace.Honor means more than just trusting Him to do it. It means without questioning. It is doing what He asks with confidence that He is working beyond what you can think or ask. Honor and service...the way to double portion blessing... not because of the blessing but because we love Him as He loves us.

"Count on it: The day is coming, raging like a forest fire. All the arrogant people who do evil things will be burned up like stove wood, burned to a crisp, nothing left but scorched earth and ash—a black day. But for you, sunrise! The sun of righteousness will dawn on those who honor my name, healing radiating from its wings. You will be bursting with energy, like colts frisky and frolicking. And you'll tromp on the wicked. They'll be nothing but ashes under your feet on that Day." God-of-the-Angel-Armies says so. "Remember and keep the revelation I gave through my servant Moses, the revelation I commanded at Horeb for all Israel, all the rules and procedures for right living.

Malachi 4: 1-3

GOOD THINGS...BAD PEOPLE!

I was asked the question as to why good things happen for bad people and bad things happen to good people. Or in essence, if God is a good God why does He allow such things as atrocities to His children like the recent murder of innocent children at a Christian school. The truth is something we value: free will. It hurts to think about it but God allows free will and choices because we choose to live in sin. A sweet friend of mine and her husband were out to dinner with their grown children and as they left the restaurant they were approached by a man asking for a ride home. They felt like this was an appropriate thing to do and an opportunity to minister to him. We will never know the full truth this side of Heaven but their lives on Earth were cut short as he murdered them and burned them in their car. Why? I have no idea. What glory did that bring to God? I have no idea. All I know is that Evil exists and permeates this Earth. Children are abused daily. Bad things happen all the time and if we think constantly on these things, we walk around burdened and heavy. Yes, we mourn and He comforts. But I do not believe we can ever understand why. My brother was murdered by a teenage classmate. I know what you feel. I have two cousins who died a senseless death in an airplane crash because of someone being careless about fueling the plane. Many many unsettling tragedies happen and if we put our eyes on the waves of evil and tragedy that are getting higher and higher, we will falter and drown in sorrow. In Malachi, God said-Count on it: the day is coming! The day of judgment for all that evil that has befallen is coming. The senselessness and evil portend of loss done by those who embraced evil will end, and the purifying fire of God will burn the arrogant people who did these things and allowed these things to a crisp. But for us who dwell in the place of refuge in the Almighty, it will be the dawn of a new day-Sonrise! The sun of righteousness will dawn on those who honor His name (hold fast without wavering or questioning despite the circumstances). His promise is that we will experience healing radiating from the wings of the dawn. We will burst with energy and feel no pain as we triumph with God. This is the blessed Hope. God says, "Count on it"! So why do good things happen now to bad people? Because the Earth has been corrupted by sin and evil has reign in the hearts and minds of many. From those who feel the power and might of their money and fame to those who are heavily burdened in sin, God still has extreme love despite the coverage of sin which He cannot abide. I know the power of bitterness and pain and I know the power of forgiveness is greater. As long as we are on Earth, there will be evil but God will catch His bride away and then He will battle the evil, destroy it once and for all then He will reign in a new Heaven and Earth with those who kept the faith. Do not let the evil waves of the world drown you in your sorrow. Reach up to Him and allow Him to lift you to walking on the waters, trodding that evil underneath you. We can look at tragedy and ache for those who experienced it but we can also know, they are celebrating at the throne of God. Those sweet teachers and children, my brother and cousins, my friend and her husband...all those who have lived and we have lost to tragedy...of any kind... they stepped from pain and misery into glory. There is no regret there. They would experience it again without hesitation if it meant the gain of what they are doing now. These moments of life are fleeting and only what we do for God will last. We are His handiwork and in the midst of tragedy, we must look to Him. Ours is not to reason why, ours is but to Trust Him on High. I know the Peace speaker. I know Him by name. If you would like an introduction, I am happy to pray with you.

Doormats of Pride!

Proverbs 29:21-23, 25 NKJV & The Message

Has anger, pride and fear driven you away from realizing your role as a child of God?

How can you protect yourself from being affected by this?

Key thought for today:

Stir Up the Gift!

II Timothy 1:6-7, 13-14

God didn't give us a spirit of fear, but....

How do you keep your "gift" fresh and on fire?

Key thought for today:

The Gate!

John 10:6-10

Jesus is our gate of....

All who enter will be....

Key thought for today:

From Plodding to Praising!

Romans 5:9-11

Define plodding:

Define praising:

What does Friendship with God mean to you?

Key thought for today:

The God Who Is, Was, Coming!

Revelation 1:4-8

We should be in breathless anticipation, celebrating, preparing, announcing and sharing with the world. Who have you told? Who do you want to tell? Why haven't you told them? Why are you waiting?

How can you spread the word?

Key thought for today:

Lost Touch!

Ephesians 4:17-19, 29

Who is God?

Do you doubt his ability or do you doubt His "want to"?

Are you stuck looking at the waves and the situation surrounding you and you've lost touch with who He is?

Key thought for today:

Build Up!

Jude 1:20-21

Have you let the fire in your life burn out?

Are you drawing from other's flames or are you using the materials God has supplied for you?

Key thought for today:

Morning's Wings!

Psalms 139:7-12

Is there any place you can go and be out of God's presence?

Why would we want to avoid God's Spirit or to be out of His sight?

Key thought for today:

Provoked Agitation!

Galatians 1:6-9

Agitated =

How can we avoid being deceived by the wiles of the devil?

Are you daily washing in the Living Water, so that you will be wise through the Holy Spirit?

Key thought for today:

Elaborate Plans!

Proverbs 16:1-3, 7-9

Are you committed to God and His plan for your life?

Why do we try and do things our own way? Where does that take us?

Key thought for today:

Dissimulation!

Romans 12:9-10

What does it mean to love without dissimulation?

How do we achieve this?

Key thought for today:

The Unclouded Day!

Psalms 139:23-24

Are you willing to trust God in every situation of your life?

Is there something today that you need to let God have control over?

Key thought for today:

Refreshed and Restored!

Jeremiah 31:21-22, 25

Has the road you've been on taken you where you don't really want to be?

How long will you wander around? Come Home.

Key thought for today:

Animated and Motivated!

Galatians 5:16-18

Why not choose to be led by the Spirit and have complete confidence in who you are in Christ?

Where are you rooted?

Key thought for today:

Deep Drafts!

Psalms 42:1-11

Are you spiritually thirsty, in need of a soul regenerating revival? What is the key?

Key thought for today:

The Secret to Happiness!

Philippians 4:10-14

What is the secret to happiness?

How can we be content in Christ Jesus?

Key thought for today:

The Model!

3 John 1:11

Be The Good =

Be the difference =

Key thought for today:

Soaked Laundry!

Psalms 51:7-15

What does a complete and thorough soaking do for our spiritual life?

How do we prepare for this?

Key thought for today:

All's Said and Done!

Joel 2:13-14

God is calling us to make a complete change in our lives, how often is this recommended?

Will you be ready when all is said and done?

Key thought for today:

Questions??

Amos 3:3-8

Signs and wonders surround us and yet the world is ignoring them, are you staying tuned in to God's voice and readying for the coming day?

What are some things you have seen/heard about that tell you His return is imminent?

Key thought for today:

Far Flung!

Amos 5:7-9, 14, 21-24

When was the last time you sang to Him?

When is the last time you spent time focused only on Him?

We like to say that God is our best friend but do we live like it? What does God want from us?

Key thought for today:

Word Hungry!

Amos 8:11-12

Are you fully relying on "Apps" or do you use a physical Bible to read and study the word of God?

If you were placed in a position where you had access to nothing, would you be able to rely on your memory from what you've studied? Have you accessed it enough that it is hidden in your heart?

Key thought for today:

A Mere Touch!

Amos 9:5-6

With one touch of His hand the earth will tremble. The King is preparing a place for His children in His palace in the skies. Are you ready? Have you fully committed your heart and life to Him?

Pray for those who need to have a fresh touch from God in their life.

Key thought for today:

I Knew It!

Jonah 4:1-2

What is your Jonah issue that is holding you back from being all that God desires for you?

Are you struggling with anger at God for not giving you the child, spouse, job, career or other that you desire?

Are you angry because you feel He blesses others and not you?

Are you frustrated and howling because He hasn't healed or performed the miracle you wanted for yourself or your family member?

Key thought for today:

Boomerang Fire!

Obadiah 1:15-18

Esau made a foolish decision, when he sold his birthright, why is this so important for us to know?

I never want to be hated by God so what must I do to make sure that I am never in that place?

Key thought for today:

Declaring Victory!

Psalms 91:1-13

When are declarations of victory declared?

Why is it so hard to stand when we are facing life's battles?

Is God able? Is He willing? Is He on time?

Key thought for today:

Juggernaut!

Micah 4:13

Juggernaut: "A force to be reckoned with that is superior in all ways-the best of the best of the best".

How can we become the juggernaut that God wants us to be?

Key thought for today:

Dead End!

Luke 9:23-27

It's really easy to want to give up sometimes and drop our hands in frustration and walk away from our situations. Why is it, that in the moment, it is so hard to trust?

Key thought for today:

Purged and Selected!

Micah 5:7

How do you usually react when you are feeling the pressure of being purged by His hand?

If you change your perception on how you look at things, does that make a difference in how your situation impacts your life?

Key thought for today:

Attention!

Micah 6:8-9

What is God looking for in men and women?

How do we do this?

Key thought for today:

Counting on God!

Micah 7:7

Why does God instruct us to put our trust only in Him, no matter what?

God knows the intricacies and details of our situations and has already planned a way of escape or refreshment; How do we stand strong and trust Him to make things right for us?

Key thought for today:

Desperate Trouble!

Nahum 1:7-10

Who do we rely on during the impossible? Is this the time we are desperate for Him?

Key thought for today:

Write This!

Habakkuk 2:1-3

Do you ever wonder why things happen or ask why God allows them?

So what is God going to say to your questions and complaints?

Key thought for today:

King of the Mountain!

Habakkuk 3:17-19

Even if things don't go as we want and desire them to go, what should we be doing?

Our confidence in Him grows as we become more intimate with Him; When we walk tall in confidence, what does this do to those who see us?

Key thought for today:

Ready or Not...Here I Come!

Zephaniah 1:7-18

God has been seeking and finding us since Jesus declared "It Is Finished" on the cross; So, why is it so hard for men and women to answer His call?

Key thought for today:

Quiet Discipline!

Zephaniah 2:1-3

Have or do you spend time soaking in His presence?

Seek Him, seek Him wholeheartedly and learn of His ways.

Key thought for today:

God's Promise!

Zephaniah 3:18-20

Are you soaking in the rain and getting wet, miserable and whiny or are you dancing in the mud puddles of promise knowing He's got it all covered in His promises?

How long has it been since you joyfully splashed in His promises without regard for your circumstances?

Key thought for today:

Joy Stealers!

Psalms 97:11

Have you opened the door to the joy stealers? They will try to come at you everyday, but you belong to Him and he is ready to help you fend them off, it's up to you to choose your weapon. What will it be?

Key thought for today:

Think it Over!

Haggai 1:5-7

What are you investing in?

How are you investing in those around you?

Where are you placing your values?

What are you doing to tell others of Christ?

Are you spreading life or are you spreading death? What are your words and deeds doing to those who surround you?

Key thought for today:

Get to Work!

Haggai 2:4-5

Have you gotten so contented with what you have that you fail to see the blessings in your life?

Are you more concerned about your don't haves than the blessings you do have?

Key thought for today:

Come Back!

Zechariah 1:1-6

What did the prophet mean when he said " Don't be like your parents"?

Why is it such a struggle to listen and obey His calling?

Key thought for today:

God's Move!

Zechariah 2:13

What is it about the quietness that prepares us to listen to His voice?

When was the last time you took time to listen? How did God speak to you or what did He show you?

Key thought for today:

If!

Zechariah 3:6-10

Which "IF" mentality are you living in? It's your choice.

Key thought for today:

What Do You See?

Zechariah 4:2-3, 8-14

What is a vision?

Are you so foggy in your vision that you fail to see God in the small things?

What is the value of that one moment? That one photo? That one second of time? What is the value of one?

What do you see?

Key thought for today:

The Book of Time Flies!

Zechariah 5:1-4

Are you making choices based upon the principles of God's word?

Who and what are you living for?

Is your name in the "Lambs Book of Life"?
We only have one life to live, what is the purpose of our life?

Key thought for today:

The People Message!

Zechariah 7:4-10

When we hold revivals or days of fasting or other religious activities, we need to examine the why. Is it out of habit or love?

Is it out of habit, expectations or love that you attend church?

What are you doing to Love your neighbors? How are you demonstrating His compassion to others?

Are you growing or are you just standing, waiting on the winds to blow you?

Key thought for today:

God's Say....!

Zechariah 8:6

Do your problems seem too much?
Is there anything too much for Him or is it because we quit asking?
What does God say?

List some of the names of God that you say He is to you:

Key thought for today:

Shine! Shimmer! Glow!

Zechariah 9:14-17

How would you describe serving God? Is it a lot of work?

Are you fully trusting in Him?

How are you preparing to be His bride?

Key thought for today:

Undeterred!

Zechariah 10:1-5

How do you keep from getting deterred when you're feeling discouraged and the weight seems too much to bear, what is the first thing you do?

What does God promise to do, if you will call on Him?

Key thought for today:

War Bulletin!

Zechariah 12:1-2

Are you listening and paying attention to the warnings from God?

In this warning, How did God say He would protect Judah and Jerusalem?

Key thought for today:

Refining Fire!

Zechariah 13:7-9

What is the refining process you are experiencing? Are you becoming more pliable in the Master Jeweler's hand or are you fighting the process?

What kind of masterpiece will you become? Have you yielded to Him?

Key thought for today:

Continuous Day!

Zechariah 14:6-9

Day stands for:

Have you lost the joy and excitement of anticipation of the day of His return? Or are you Contagious?

Key thought for today:

Angel Armies!

Malachi 1:11, 14

Honor =

Where is His honor?
Are you sacrificing the waiting time of hours in His word and worship in anticipation of what He will do when you enter the House of God? Are you giving God your best or is He getting leftovers? Are you prioritizing God and giving Him quality time, effort and gifts?

Key thought for today:

The Faith-Bond!

Malachi 2:13-15

When was the last time you took measure of your faith bond? Are you heeding the still small voice warning you that there are areas you must address? Are you busy whining that things aren't going the way you want but have ignored the person you vowed to prioritize?

Would God be pleased with how you are honoring the faith bond you pledged before Him?

Key thought for today:

To Honor is to Serve!

Malachi 3:5, 17-18

What does it mean to serve with honor?

If we serve a God who was willing to give up everything to serve us, then why are we not willing to honor him in our service? Why do we question his authority?

Key thought for today:

Good things...Bad People!

Malachi 4:1-3

What is free will?

What is the blessed hope?

So, why do good things happen now to bad people?

Key thought for today: